CHRIST'S
SOVEREIGNTY

"2 I am the LORD thy [Your] God, which have brought thee [you] out of the land of Egypt" (Exodus 20:2).

By: Philip Mitanidis

Dedicated to: Katherine

Copyright © 2017 by Philip Mitanidis
All Rights Reserved

All rights reserved. No part of this publication may be reproduced or transmitted in any form or by any means, electronically, or mechanically, including photocopy, recording, or by any information storage and retrieving system without written permission from the publisher.

For further information or request for permission to make copies of any part of the work should be in a written form and mailed to the following address:

BEEHIVE PUBLISHING HOUSE INC.
www.beehivepublishinghouse.com
email: info@beehivepublishinghouse.com

CHRIST'S SOVEREIGNTY
First Edition 2017 Printed in the USA
ISBN 978-0-9866246-9-8

Published works by the author:
- The Creator of Genesis 1:1—Who is He?
- The Covenant—A contract Rejected
- No God and Saviour Beside Me
- According to a Promise
- Christians Headed into the Time of Trouble
- Ghosts Demons UFO'S and Dead Men
- Moses Wrote About Me
- What is the Sign of Christ's Second Coming and the End of the World
- The Sign in Matthew 24
- Is Apostle John Still Alive Today?
- Christ's Sovereignty

ACKNOWLEDGMENT & ABBREVIATIONS......v

All Scripture is quoted from the Old King James Version (OKJV) of the Bible, unless otherwise stated.

I have placed in brackets "[ ]" words or a word to clarify the meaning of the preceding word in some references, which I have quoted from the Old King James Version (OKJV) of the Bible. I also have translated the Hebrew word "יהוה" and the Greek word "Κυριος" to read "LORD" whenever the Scriptures refer to God the Creator of Genesis 1:1. Furthermore, I capitalized the first letter of the pronouns, which refer to God the Creator of Genesis 1:1.

Please refer to the Hebrew and to the Greek inspired Scriptures in order to verify my opinions.

Greek Scriptures are taken from: Η Αγια Γραφη, Βιβλικη Εταιρεια, Αθηναι, 1961.

Front Cover and artwork in this book are produced by the Author Philip Mitanidis.

FOREWORD

The Sovereign God of our universe and outside of our universe says,

> "4 Yet I am the LORD thy [Your] God from the land of Egypt, and thou [you] shalt know no god but Me" (Hosea 13:4).

When you read the above verse, who do you think says, "4 Yet I am the LORD thy [Your] God from the land of Egypt"?
Is He the God of the Jews?
Is He the God of the Muslims?
Or, is He the God of the Christians?

As you probably already know, there are three religious groups, which make up over three and a half billion people on planet earth; and each group identifies itself by the name of Jews, Muslims, or Christians. And these individuals who are affiliated with their respective religious institutions (Synagogues, Mosques, and Christian churches) use the Bible, to one degree or another, to form their religious doctrines.

But, more precisely, these three humongous religious institutions use their respective prophets and parts of the Bible to form their religious doctrines, and discard other parts of the Bible. Consequently, they continue to disagree with each other's religious doctrines, even though their dialogue, amongst them, centers around the Torah (the five books of Moses). And, in one of those religious doctrinal points, which is said to be formed from the writings of the Torah, is somewhat stated in variance, in one form or another, by these three humongous religious institutions. They claim the Sovereign God of "all things," the universe, and outside of the universe, is "God the Father," as we know him now in the New Testament (NT).

Although the Jews (the House of Judah) believe that the Sovereign God of the Torah is none other than the God of Abraham, many individuals today refrain from using the name "God the Father," when referring to the God of Abraham because that would imply that God the Father had a Son. And the Son would be, as per Scripture (New and Old Testaments), the Messiah (Christ John 1:41), which they deny. They reject Christ as the Messiah even though He fulfilled all of the Messianic Scripture references, which foretold of His coming in the flesh.

The attitude and rejection of Jesus Christ the LORD today is the same as it was during Christ's time; some individuals believed in Christ discreetly because they feared persecution from the Jewish authorities. Others, even though the Jewish authorities persecuted them, they remained believers in Christ openly before the public. In fact, some like the apostles first went about preaching Jesus Christ crucified and resurrected to the House of Judah; and when the House of Judah rejected Christ's atoning sacrifice for their sins, the apostles went and preached to the Gentiles.

Here are few references to the above facts:

> "[37] And the two disciples heard him speak, and they followed Jesus. [38] Then Jesus turned, and saw them following, and saith unto them, What seek ye? They said unto Him, Rabbi, (which is

to say, being interpreted, Master,) where dwellest thou [You]? 39 He saith unto them, Come and see. They came and saw where He dwelt, and abode with Him that day: for it was about the tenth hour.

"40 One of the two which heard John speak, and followed Him, was Andrew, Simon Peter's brother.

"41 He first findeth his own brother Simon, and saith unto him, We have found the Messias, which is, being interpreted, the Christ.

"42 And he brought him to Jesus. And when Jesus beheld him, He said, Thou [you] art Simon the son of Jona: thou [you] shalt be called Cephas, which is by interpretation, A stone. 43 The day following Jesus would go forth into Galilee, and findeth Philip, and saith unto him, Follow Me.

"44 Now Philip was of Bethsaida, the city of Andrew and Peter. 45 Philip findeth Nathanael, and saith unto him, We have found Him, of whom Moses in the law, and the prophets, did write, Jesus of Nazareth, the son of Joseph.

"46 And Nathanael said unto him, Can there any good thing come out of Nazareth? Philip saith unto him, Come and see. 47 Jesus saw Nathanael coming to Him, and saith of him, Behold an Israelite indeed, in whom is no guile! 48 Nathanael saith unto Him, Whence knowest thou me? Jesus answered and said unto him, Before that Philip called thee [you], when thou [you] wast under the fig tree, I saw thee.

> "49 Nathanael answered and saith unto Him, Rabbi, thou [You] art the Son of God; thou [You] art the King of Israel.

"50 Jesus answered and said unto him, Because I said unto thee [you], I saw thee under the fig tree, believest thou? thou [you] shalt see greater things than these. 51 And He saith unto him, Verily, verily, I say unto you, Hereafter ye [all of you] shall see heaven open, and the angels of God ascending and descending upon the Son of man." John 1:37-51

And after Jesus Christ the LORD successfully executed the Plan of Salvation, (died sinless on Calvary's cross and was resurrected), the apostles went about preaching Christ crucified and resurrected, first to the House of Judah and then to the Gentiles.

> "45 when the Jews saw the multitudes, they were filled with envy, and spake against those things which were spoken by Paul, contradicting and blaspheming.

> "46 Then Paul and Barnabas waxed bold, and

said, It was necessary that the word of God should first have been spoken to you: but seeing ye [all of you] put it from you, and judge yourselves unworthy of everlasting life, lo, we turn to the Gentiles." Acts 13:45, 46

As per Scripture, although many of the Jews believed Christ was the Messiah during His ministry, two thousand years ago, others like today chose not to believe in Christ. In fact because of their constant rejection of Christ, the apostles, as you have read, said to the Jews, "46 It was necessary that the word of God should first have been spoken to you: but seeing ye [all of you] put it from you, and judge yourselves unworthy of everlasting life, lo, we turn to the Gentiles" (Acts 13:46). And turned they did indeed.

Although the Jews rejected Christ, it appears that the Jews had, as they have today, formulated some kind of identity and concept of the God of Abraham because He had appeared to Abraham, Jacob, and to Moses a number of times.

Like-wise, the Muslims believe that the Sovereign God of the Torah is the God of Abraham. But, on the long run, it appears that the Muslims put the emphases on their prophet Muhammad by placing the name Muhammad before their given names; whereby, the Jews simply claim that they are the children of their father Abraham (John 8:53). And like the Jewish believers, the Muslims refrain from using the name "God the Father" as the Sovereign God because they say and teach that their God "does not have a Son." Therefore, they, like the Jews, refer to him as the God of Abraham.

On the other hand, many of the Muslims admit

and acknowledge, on the overall that they do not have an image of the God of Abraham, which is portrayed in the Torah. It is claimed that their God is "unimaginable" (Translators notes page 1. Qur'an. MMP.)

The problem with religious institutions, which claim that their god is indescribable or "unimaginable," is the fact that it places them in an awkward position because by disclaiming the identity of their god, they cannot identify or relate to their god. And by not knowing to whom or to what they are praying to, it places their god and their prayers into oblivion.

By saying that your god is indescribable and "unimaginable," and by admitting that you do not know what He looks like, it brings about a number of ramifications upon yourself and upon the Torah. In fact, it brings about a number of implications to the entire Bible. And at the end, the religious doctrines of men become combatant with the doctrine of the Bible.

By saying that your god is "unimaginable," you are also denying the Scripture references that are provided in the Bible, by the prophets of old, which clearly describe His identity and the Sovereignty of the God of Abraham.

Having said that, it should be noted; although the Jews, Muslims, and a handful of Christian religious institutions pick and choose what portions of the Bible they want to believe, in order to support their religious doctrine; it is sad to report, even the majority of the Evangelical Christian belief's have been duped to believe like the Greek Orthodox Church, Roman Catholic Church, Jews, and Muslims that God the Father is the Sovereign God of "all things." This claim is clearly stated by their modern day prophets and in their Catechisms, under "The Apostle's Creed."

And to support their claim, of the superiority of God the Father, they quote, as an example; the following mistranslated verses, which state that somebody created the all things "through Him [Christ]" (Colossians 1:16; John 1:3, 10). And by using the uninspired added word "through" in the New Testament creation verses, the New Testament creation verses are made to posture and contradict all of the creation verses in the Old Testament. None of the creation verses of the Hebrew text, in the Old Testament, state or suggests that somebody created something or the "all things" "through" Jesus Christ or "through" someone else?

It should be noticed, the mistranslated word "through" does not exist in these creation verses of the Old and New Testaments. The Greek word is "δι' " (by). Therefore, the Greek references, in all of these creation verses, in the New Testament, read, "all things were created by [δι'] Him [Christ]." (More on this point later.)

Therefore, as per Scripture, we can conclude, all of the above humongous religious institutions disagree with the Bible prophets, when they clearly state, in their writings that the Sovereign God of "all things" is not God the Father.

So! How did over three and a half billion people, from all walks of life, become so drastically duped and mislead to believe that God the Father is the Sovereign God of "all things"?

Do you know?

The Author.

CONTENTS

v	Acknowledgements and Abbreviations
vi	Foreword
13.	Contents
14.	Memorandum
15.	No God Beside Me
35.	One God or More?
55.	One God vs. the Trinity
74.	Identifying the God of Abraham and of Israel.
107.	Meeting with the God of Abraham and of Israel
126.	At Kadesh-barnea
137.	Crossing the Jordan River into Gilgal
157.	In the Promised Land
170.	Claiming Sovereignty
199.	Supplements
	1 Corinthians 15:28
210.	Questions

Memorandum   To those individuals who believe, there is only one God mentioned in the Bible, and to those who believe, there are three independent Gods mentioned in the Bible, and to those who believe, there are three Gods in one body, this book is written to identify and confirm Biblically who is the God of Abraham and of the children of Israel; and who is the Individual claiming Sovereignty over "all things" by saying "there is no God beside Me"?

In order to identify who is the God of Abraham and of the children of Israel, and who claims that there is "no God beside Me," I have taken a number of sequential events from the Torah (the 5 books of Moses) as a prerequisite reading. And, I am going to use these sequential references from the Torah, to confirm the cross-reference facts that are stated by the other prophets of the LORD. All of these references, reveal the identity of the "God of Abraham and of Israel." And they also reveal who is the Sovereign God of "all things" who says,

> "2 I am the LORD thy [Your] God, which have brought thee [you] out of the land of Egypt." Exodus 20:2

If you have never read the Torah, you will find that it is a good way to become familiar with the Hebrews, better known as the children of Israel (Jacob), with their history, with the "LORD God of Abraham and of Israel," and who makes the statement, "there is no God beside Me," and who claims to be the Sovereign God of "all things."

No God Beside Me

It is a well-known fact in the religious world that the majority of Jews, Muslims, and a handful of Christian denominations, which believe in the Bible, acknowledge that there is only "one God." On the other hand, the majority of Christian denominations, such as the Greek Orthodox Church, Roman Catholic Church, and the Protestant churches claim to believe that there are three Gods—God the Christ, God the Father, and God the Holy Spirit as we know them in the New Testament (NT)—mentioned in the Bible by the names of "LORD God." But contrary to their belief, one of these three Individuals has taken upon Himself to boldly proclaim to all of the people, who read the Bible that there is no God beside Him!

And that claim, by the Sovereign LORD God of "all things" that there is no God beside Him, and that He is the LORD God of Abraham and of Israel, has created quite a controversial stir amongst all of these religious institutions by Him saying,

> "5 I am the LORD, and there is none else,"

And again, He says,

> "there is no God beside Me" (Isaiah 45:5).

Christ's Sovereignty......... *By: Philip Mitanidis*
No God Beside Me

How can one of the three Gods of the Bible (God the Christ, God the Father, God the Holy Spirit), in the light of Scripture, make contradictory statements like that?
Or, are they contradictory?
What do you think?
Are the above bold statements contradictory?
If so, is He lying to us?
But, if He is not lying to us, how does He justify His claims?
Perhaps the above statements are mistranslated from the Hebrew Scriptures; but, if they are not mistranslated, are they still conflicting?
If you say that the above statements are not contradictory, I have to ask why not?
On the other hand, if you do find the above statements contradictory, we have to ask, why is He saying "there is no God beside Me"?
Since the LORD God of Abraham and of Israel continues to stand firm on His statement, which says, "there is no God beside Me," it sends a message to us that He is the Sovereign God of "all things."
Therefore let us consider the following presentations and Scripture references, and see the outcome as to why He is saying "there is no God beside Me" when Scripture clearly reveals three separate Individuals by the name of "LORD God."
Speaking to Cyrus the Persian King, who was going to defeat the Babylonian king, with the LORD'S help, and inherit the children of Israel, who were going to be taken captive for seventy years by the Chaldeans, this is what the LORD God of Israel said,

No God Beside Me

"1 to His anointed, to Cyrus, whose right hand I have holden, to subdue nations before him; and I will loose the loins of kings, to open before him the two leaved gates; and the gates shall not be shut;

"2 I will go before thee [you], and make the crooked places straight: I will break in pieces the gates of brass, and cut in sunder the bars of iron: 3 And I will give thee [you] the treasures of darkness, and hidden riches of secret places, that thou [you] mayest know that I, the LORD, which call thee [you] by thy [your] name, am the God of Israel. 4 For Jacob My servant's sake, and Israel mine elect, I have even called thee [you] by thy [your] name: I have surnamed thee [you], though thou [you] hast not known Me." Isaiah 45:1-4

According to the above presentation, even though Cyrus does not know the LORD God of Israel ("thou [you] hast not known Me" v.4), the LORD God of Israel and of Abraham still revealed the above prophetic events to the children of Israel and to Cyrus that Cyrus would come to power, defeat the Babylonians, and liberate the children of Israel from their seventy years of captivity that would be held by the Babylonians, so that they can return to the Promised Land. He said to Cyrus,

"5 I am the LORD, and there is none else, there is no God beside Me:

Christ's Sovereignty……….. *By: Philip Mitanidis*
No God Beside Me

"I girded thee [you], though thou [you] hast not known Me: 6 That they may know from the rising of the sun, and from the west, that there is none beside Me.

"I am the LORD, and there is none else."
Isaiah 45:5, 6

Very strong statements don't you think that there is only one God ("there is none else" v.6)?

But, the LORD'S statement to Cyrus that "there is no God beside Me," was not the only time it was echoed throughout Israel. In reference to the God of Israel, King Solomon during his dedication prayer for the newly built Sanctuary in Jerusalem also acknowledged that there is "no God like thee [You], in heaven above, or on earth beneath." And in reference to the God he was praying to, Solomon acknowledged that He is the "LORD God of Israel."

Here are the references:

"22 And Solomon stood before the altar of the LORD in the presence of all the congregation of Israel, and spread forth his hands toward heaven:

"23 And he said, LORD God of Israel, there is no God like thee [You], in heaven above, or on earth beneath,

"who keepest covenant and mercy with thy

No God Beside Me

[Your] servants that walk before thee [You] with all their heart: 24 Who hast kept with thy [Your] servant David my father that thou [You] promisedst him: thou [You] spakest also with thy [Your] mouth, and hast fulfilled it with thine [Your] hand, as it is this day.

"25 Therefore now, LORD God of Israel, keep with thy [Your] servant David my father that thou [You] promisedst him, saying, There shall not fail thee a man in My sight to sit on the throne of Israel; so that thy [your] children take heed to their way, that they walk before Me as thou [you] hast walked before Me.

"26 And now, O God of Israel, let thy [Your] word, I pray thee [You], be verified, which thou [You] spakest unto thy [Your] servant David my father.

"27 But will God indeed dwell on the earth? behold, the heaven and heaven of heavens cannot contain thee; how much less this house that I have builded?" 1 Kings 8:22-27

    In the above presentation, King Solomon acknowledges that the God of Israel is one of a kind God by saying; there is "23 no God like thee [You], in heaven above, or on earth beneath."
    And in reference to this very same God, King Solomon says that His whole creation cannot contain

No God Beside Me

Him (v.27).

Can you imagine the above statement that the whole creation cannot contain Him? That means the whole universe and outside of the universe cannot contain the LORD God of Israel.

And, by saying that there is "no God like thee [You], in heaven above, or on earth beneath," King Solomon acknowledges that he was referring to and praying to the one LORD God of Israel and of Abraham.

Like-wise, in reference to Naaman who was afflicted with leprosy, when,

> "9 Naaman came with his horses and with his chariot, and stood at the door of the house of Elisha. 10 And Elisha sent a messenger unto him, saying,
>
>> "Go and wash in Jordan seven times, and thy [your] flesh shall come again to thee, and thou [you] shalt be clean.
>
> "11 But Naaman was wroth, and went away, and said, Behold, I thought, He will surely come out to me, and stand, and call on the name of the LORD his God, and strike his hand over the place, and recover the leper. 12 Are not Abana and Pharpar, rivers of Damascus, better than all the waters of Israel? may I not wash in them, and be clean? So he turned and went away in a rage.

No God Beside Me

"13 And his servants came near, and spake unto him, and said, My father, if the prophet had bid thee [you] do some great thing, wouldest thou [you] not have done it? how much rather then, when he saith to thee [you], Wash, and be clean?

"14 Then went he down, and dipped himself seven times in Jordan, according to the saying of the man of God: and his flesh came again like unto the flesh of a little child, and he was clean.

"15 And he returned to the man of God, he and all his company, and came, and stood before him: and he said,

> "Behold, now I know that there is no God in all the earth, but in Israel:

"now therefore, I pray thee [you, Elisha], take a blessing of thy [your] servant. 16 But he said, As the LORD liveth, before whom I stand, I will receive none. And he urged him to take it; but he refused." 2 Kings 5:9-16

After Naaman got mad at Elisha, the prophet of the LORD, for not telling him to go and wash in one of the two local rivers, and for not performing something spectacular or unusual, such as chanting, jumping up and down five thousand times, or begging to be healed from his leprosy, eventually, after receiving his servants advice, he repented and did as Elisha told him to do;

No God Beside Me

and that was to go and wash in the Jordan River. He was to wash himself seven times. And when Naaman did that, he was cured. And after he was cured, he acknowledged that there was no God on earth except in Israel.

Naaman made that remark because like many people of today who are sick and lost hope in men's medicine, voodoo, and satanic rituals, to cure them, by going to the LORD God of Israel, as he did, they can be cured. And therefore, like Naaman they can conclude and make that very same statement,

> "15 now I know that there is no God in all the earth, but in Israel." 2 Kings 5:15

Hezekiah like Naaman acknowledges that the LORD God of Israel is the only God by saying, "thou [You] art the LORD God, even thou [You] only."

Here are the references, which caused Hezekiah, under belligerent conditions, to exclaim, "thou [You] art the LORD God, even thou [You] only."

"17 And the king of Assyria sent Tartan and Rabsaris and Rabshakeh from Lachish to king Hezekiah with a great host against Jerusalem. And they went up and came to Jerusalem. And when they were come up, they came and stood by the conduit of the upper pool, which is in the highway of the fuller's field. 18 And when they had called to the king, there came out to them Eliakim the son of Hilkiah, which was over the household, and Shebna the scribe, and Joah the son of Asaph the recorder.

"19 And Rabshakeh said unto them, Speak ye now to Hezekiah, Thus saith the great king, the king of

No God Beside Me

Assyria, What confidence is this wherein thou [you] trustest? 20 Thou [you] sayest, (but they are but vain words,) I have counsel and strength for the war. Now on whom dost thou [you] trust, that thou rebellest against me? 21 Now, behold, thou trustest upon the staff of this bruised reed, even upon Egypt, on which if a man lean, it will go into his hand, and pierce it: so is Pharaoh king of Egypt unto all that trust on him. 22 But if ye say unto me, We trust in the LORD our God: is not that he, whose high places and whose altars Hezekiah hath taken away, and hath said to Judah and Jerusalem, Ye [all of you] shall worship before this altar in Jerusalem? 23 Now therefore, I pray thee, give pledges to my lord the king of Assyria, and I will deliver thee two thousand horses, if thou [you] be able on thy [your] part to set riders upon them. 24 How then wilt thou [you] turn away the face of one captain of the least of my master's servants, and put thy [your] trust on Egypt for chariots and for horsemen? 25 Am I now come up without the LORD against this place to destroy it? The LORD said to me, Go up against this land, and destroy it.

> "26 Then said Eliakim the son of Hilkiah, and Shebna, and Joah, unto Rabshakeh, Speak, I pray thee, to thy servants in the Syrian language; for we understand it: and talk not with us in the Jews' language in the ears of the people that are on the wall.
>
> > "27 But Rabshakeh said unto them, Hath my master sent me to thy [your] master, and to thee

No God Beside Me

[you], to speak these words? hath he not sent me to the men which sit on the wall, that they may eat their own dung, and drink their own piss with you?

"28 Then Rabshakeh stood and cried with a loud voice in the Jews' language, and spake, saying, Hear the word of the great king, the king of Assyria: 29 Thus saith the king, Let not Hezekiah deceive you: for he shall not be able to deliver you out of his hand: 30 Neither let Hezekiah make you trust in the LORD, saying, The LORD will surely deliver us, and this city shall not be delivered into the hand of the king of Assyria. 31 Hearken not to Hezekiah: for thus saith the king of Assyria, Make an agreement with me by a present, and come out to me, and then eat ye every man of his own vine, and every one of his fig tree, and drink ye every one the waters of his cistern: 32 Until I come and take you away to a land like your own land, a land of corn and wine, a land of bread and vineyards, a land of oil olive and of honey, that ye may live, and not die: and hearken not unto Hezekiah, when he persuadeth you, saying, The LORD will deliver us. 33 Hath any of the gods of the nations delivered at all his land out of the hand of the king of Assyria? 34 Where are the gods of Hamath, and of Arpad? where are the gods of Sepharvaim, Hena, and Ivah? have they delivered Samaria out of mine hand? 35 Who are they among all the gods of the countries, that have delivered their country out of mine hand, that the LORD should deliver Jerusalem out of mine hand?

"36 But the people held their peace, and

No God Beside Me

answered him not a word: for the king's commandment was, saying, Answer him not.

"37 Then came Eliakim the son of Hilkiah, which was over the household, and Shebna the scribe, and Joah the son of Asaph the recorder, to Hezekiah with their clothes rent, and told him the words of Rabshakeh." 2 Kings 18:17-37

Hezekiah's prayer took place during the time when the people in Jerusalem were terrified by the words of Sennacherib the king of Assyria.

Therefore Hezekiah prayed to the LORD God of Israel saying,

> "15 And Hezekiah prayed before the LORD, and said, O LORD God of Israel, which dwellest between the cherubims, thou [You] art the God, even thou [You] alone, of all the kingdoms of the earth; thou [You] hast made heaven and earth.

> "16 LORD, bow down thine ear, and hear: open, LORD, thine eyes, and see: and hear the words of Sennacherib, which hath sent him to reproach the living God. 17 Of a truth, LORD, the kings of Assyria have destroyed the nations and their lands, 18 And have cast their gods into the fire: for they were no gods, but the work of men's hands, wood and stone: therefore they have destroyed them. 19 Now therefore, O LORD our God, I beseech thee, save thou [You] us out of his hand,

> "that all the kingdoms of the

earth may know that thou [You] art the LORD God, even thou [You] only.

"20 Then Isaiah the son of Amoz sent to Hezekiah, saying, Thus saith the LORD God of Israel, That which thou [you] hast prayed to Me against Sennacherib king of Assyria I have heard. 21 This is the word that the LORD hath spoken concerning him; The virgin the daughter of Zion hath despised thee [you], and laughed thee to scorn; the daughter of Jerusalem hath shaken her head at thee [you]. 22 Whom hast thou [you] reproached and blasphemed? and against whom hast thou [you] exalted thy [your] voice, and lifted up thine [your] eyes on high? even against the Holy One of Israel." 2 Kings 19:15-22

It should be noticed, in verse twenty above, the LORD God of Israel identifies Himself by the use of the single pronouns "Me" ("thou [you] hast prayed to Me") and "I" ("I have heard") to indicate that He is not referring to more than one LORD God of Israel, or include another God beside Himself.

Isaiah said, "20 Thus saith the LORD God of Israel, That which thou [you] hast prayed to Me against Sennacherib king of Assyria I have heard."

By saying, "I have heard" Hezekiah's prayer, the LORD God of Israel delivered the children of Israel from the Assyrian king and saved the people of Israel without going to war.

Thus, according the above verses the God of

Christ's Sovereignty.......... *By: Philip Mitanidis*
No God Beside Me

Israel is identified by the prophet by saying, "thou [You] art the LORD God, even thou [You] only." And according to that statement, the LORD God of Israel is the "only" God.

And to complicate matters even more, for some people, this very same LORD God of Israel says, "there is no God with Me."

Here are the references:

> "39 See now that I, even I, am He, and there is no God with Me" (Deuteronomy 32:39).

Since the above verse clearly states that there is no God with the God of Israel, and the LORD God of Israel cannot be contained in His whole creation (1 Kings 8:27), and expands beyond His creation, where are the other two Gods that are mentioned in the Bible residing?

According to the Bible, the other two Gods reside in the third heaven, and so does the LORD God of Israel. Therefore we have to ask, why is the LORD God of Israel saying that there is no God with Him?

And even more profound, the LORD God of Israel and of Abraham not only goes one step further and says, "beside Me there is no God," but, He also questions, "Is there a God beside Me?" And then, He answers, "yea, there is no God; I know not any."

Here are the references:

> "6 Thus saith the LORD the King of Israel, and his Redeemer the LORD of hosts; I am the first,

No God Beside Me

and I am the last; and beside Me there is no God.

"7 And who, as I, shall call, and shall declare it, and set it in order for Me, since I appointed the ancient people? and the things that are coming, and shall come, let them shew unto them. 8 Fear ye not, neither be afraid: have not I told thee from that time, and have declared it?

"ye [all of you] are even My witnesses. Is there a God beside Me? yea, there is no God; I know not any." Isaiah 44:6-8

By reading the above verses, they obviously bring a number of questions to mind. Logically, since the LORD God of Israel resides in the third heaven, and the other two Gods also reside in the third heaven, we can ask, how can the God of Israel ask such extreme question by saying, "Is there a God beside Me?" and make such outlandish statements, "yea, there is no God; I know not any." Isaiah 44:8

Again, we have to ask, how can the LORD God of Israel ask, "Is there a God beside Me?"

How can He say, "I know not any"?

How can He not know if there is a God or Gods beside Him or not?

And how can He say, "I know not any" when the prophets of the Bible and He, on number of occasions, refer to two more Gods with the same name as His?

According to King Solomon, since the LORD

No God Beside Me

God of Israel and of Abraham occupies the whole universe and outside of the universe (1 Kings 8:27), we can ask, where are the other two Gods staying for the God of Israel to make such questionable statements? Or what space do they occupy that they are not acknowledged by this one God of Israel who says, "there is no God beside Me," or "with Me."

What do you think?

Are these two Gods out of sight and out of mind, is that why the LORD God of Abraham and of Israel says, "there is no God beside Me"?

If they are not out of sight and out of mind, is there another realm beyond the third heaven, which is outside of our universe that the other two Gods occupy and therefore we can conclude, they are not with the God of Israel?

If that is the case, what do these two Gods do there and what do they occupy?

But, if they are not in another realm and abide in the third heaven, as the God of Israel does, why is the LORD God of Israel saying, "there is no God beside Me"? And why are they not acknowledged, as Gods, by the Jews, Muslims, and by a handful of Christian institutions? And why are they not acknowledged as the Gods of Israel? And, why are the children of Israel claiming that the LORD God of Israel and of Abraham is their only God when the prophets of old identify and refer to two more Gods beside the LORD God of Israel?

They do because their LORD God of Israel and of Abraham has stated to them over and over again that they shalt have no other God/gods before Him. In fact, before the LORD God of Israel gave verbally the first

No God Beside Me

Commandment to the children of Israel, from the top of Mount Sinai, He introduced Himself by saying,

> "2 I am the LORD thy [Your] God, which have brought thee out of the land of Egypt, out of the house of bondage.

And then He said to them,

> "3 Thou [you] shalt have no other gods before Me" (Exodus 20:3).

Thus out of the Ten Commandments, the LORD God of Israel placed the first Commandment at the forefront as a priority. If the children of Israel would not accept the first Commandment, but accept and abide in the other nine, they would be living in sin. Therefore they had to make a choice, accept and acknowledge the first Commandment and live, or reject the first Commandment and perish (James 2:10; Romans 6:23).

Furthermore, the LORD God of Abraham and of Israel states in the second Commandment not to reject the first Commandment, or replacing the first Commandment with the second Commandment by making "any graven image, or any thing that is in heaven above, or that is in the earth beneath," and bow down to them or serve them.

The God of Israel says,

> "4 Thou [you] shalt not make unto thee any graven image, or any likeness of any thing that is in heaven above, or that is in the earth

No God Beside Me

beneath, or that is in the water under the earth: 5 Thou [you] shalt not bow down thyself to them, nor serve them: for I the LORD thy [Your] God am a jealous God, visiting the iniquity of the fathers upon the children unto the third and fourth generation of them that hate me; 6 And shewing mercy unto thousands of them that love me, and keep my commandments." Exodus 20:4-6

As per the first and second Commandments, the LORD God of Israel is clearly saying to the children of Israel and to you and to me, we are not to have other God (s) before Him. I include us because the children of Israel were to give the Ten Commandments to us the Gentiles (Acts 7:38).

For that reason, after the kingdom of King Solomon was split into two, the House of Judah, which included the 2 tribes (Benjamin and Judah) kept warning the House of Israel (Jacob), which included the ten tribes to stop praying to the two calves that were made by King Jeroboam for the ten tribes to go and worship.

The prophet of the LORD writes,

"7 And there are gathered unto him vain men, the children of Belial, and have strengthened themselves against Rehoboam the son of Solomon, when Rehoboam was young and tenderhearted, and could not withstand them. 8 And now ye think to withstand the kingdom of the LORD in the hand of the sons of David; and ye be a great multitude, and there are with you golden calves, which Jeroboam made you for gods.

Christ's Sovereignty……….. *By: Philip Mitanidis*
No God Beside Me

"9 Have ye [the 10 tribes of Israel (House of Israel)] not cast out the priests of the LORD, the sons of Aaron, and the Levites, and have made you priests after the manner of the nations of other lands? so that whosoever cometh to consecrate himself with a young bullock and seven rams, the same may be a priest of them that are no gods.

"10 But as for us [the House of Judah], the LORD is our God, and we have not forsaken Him;

"and the priests, which minister unto the LORD, are the sons of Aaron, and the Levites wait upon their business: 11 And they burn unto the LORD every morning and every evening burnt sacrifices and sweet incense: the shewbread also set they in order upon the pure table; and the candlestick of gold with the lamps thereof,

"to burn every evening: for we keep the charge of the LORD our God;

"but ye [all of you] have forsaken Him. 12 And, behold, God himself is with us for our captain, and His priests with sounding trumpets to cry alarm against you.

"O children of Israel, fight ye [all of you] not against the LORD God of your fathers; for ye [all of you] shall not prosper." 2 Chronicles 13:7-12

No God Beside Me

As you have read, the House of Judah (the two tribes) openly rebukes the House of Israel (the ten tribes of Israel) for worshiping the golden calves King Jeroboam made for them.

The House of Judah said to the house of Israel, "$_{12}$ O children of Israel, fight ye [all of you] not against the LORD God of your fathers; for ye shall not prosper." 2 Chronicles 13:12

The admonitions towards the House of Israel was to:

> "$_{11}$ keep the charge of the LORD our God" (2 Chronicles 13:11).

Did you notice; the House of Judah (Benjamin and Judah) not only directs the House of Israel to worship "the LORD God of our fathers," but also refers to Him as "the LORD our God."

So! According to the above testimony, "the LORD God of our fathers" is "the LORD our God" of the House of Judah. And the reason I am specifically referring to the LORD God of Judah because the House of Israel (ten tribes) had fallen into apostasy. They were worshipping the golden calves, which were conveniently located by Jeroboam, one in the tribe of Dan and the other in Bethel.

Nonetheless Scripture testifies by the pen of Moses when he said,

> "$_3$ Hear therefore, O Israel, and observe to do it; that it may be well with thee, and that ye [all of you] may increase mightily, as the LORD God of thy [your] fathers hath promised thee [you],

No God Beside Me

in the land that floweth with milk and honey.

> "₄ Hear, O Israel: The LORD our God is one LORD:
>
> "₅ And thou shalt love the LORD thy [your] God with all thine heart, and with all thy soul, and with all thy might.
>
> "₆ And these words, which I command thee [you] this day, shall be in thine heart" (Deuteronomy 6:3-6

As you have read in v.4, Moses emphatically stated to the children of Israel,

> "₄ Hear, O Israel: The LORD our God is one LORD."

Therefore we have to conclude, as per the result of the above references, there is only one God, as in number one (1), and that God is the LORD God of Israel and of Abraham. But, at the same time, we have to ask, why are the other two Gods of the Bible excluded, by the God of Abraham, as the Gods of the children of Israel, by saying, "there is no God beside Me"; "I know not any"?

Or, are they excluded?

What do you think; is there an answer?

ONE GOD OR MORE?

To confirm the fact that there are three Gods mentioned throughout the sixty-six books of the Bible, I am going to bring a handful of Bible verses for your consideration, which clearly reveal more than one God.

Although the verses in the previous chapter unmistakably reveal that there is one single Individual who claims that "there is no God beside Me," if you are an avid reader of the Bible, you would have noticed a number of times that there is more than one LORD God with the same name mentioned throughout the Bible.

As an example, here are few verses of many, which reveal more than one LORD and more than one God taken from the Old Testament.

> "18 And Lot said unto them, Oh, not so, my Lord: 19 Behold now, thy [your] servant hath found grace in thy sight, and thou [you] hast magnified thy mercy, which thou hast shewed unto me in saving my life; and I cannot escape to the mountain, lest some evil take me, and I die: 20 Behold now, this city is near to flee unto, and it is a little one: Oh, let me escape thither, (is it not a little one?) and my soul shall live.
>
> "21 And he said unto him, See, I have accepted thee concerning this thing also, that I will not overthrow this city, for the which thou [you] hast spoken. 22 Haste thee, escape thither; for I

One God or More?

cannot do any thing till thou be come thither. Therefore the name of the city was called Zoar. 23 The sun was risen upon the earth when Lot entered into Zoar.

"24 Then the LORD [יהוה] rained upon Sodom and upon Gomorrah brimstone and fire from the LORD [יהוה] out of heaven;

"25 And He overthrew those cities, and all the plain, and all the inhabitants of the cities, and that which grew upon the ground." Genesis 19:18-25

Lot who was approached by the two angels and advised him and his family to leave the city, he did not want to co-operate with the two angels, even when the angels asked them to hang on to each other's hands while they were leaving the city. He said to them that he did not want to go and hide in the caves of the mountain, in order to avert his and his family's destruction. Instead he insisted and said to the angels that he wanted to go and hide in the town of Zoar.

Lot, like his wife had hard time leaving the life of the perverted city. He did not want to go and find shelter in the mountains. But Lot's wife went one step further; she turned around to go back into the city, in spite of the warning that was given to her not to look back or attempt to go back in the city. As you probably know, by walking into the inferno zone, brimstone and fire fell upon her and turned her into a pillar of salt because she chose to disobey the merciful command

One God or More?

and the advice of the angels.

The record, by Moses, tells us that the LORD God of Abraham "overthrew those cities, and all the plain, and all the inhabitants of the cities, and that which grew upon the ground." It was during that time the demise of Lot's wife took place.

And how did the LORD God of Abraham overthrow the fields and the cities and the sinners of these cities?

Moses wrote,

> "24 Then the LORD [יהוה] rained upon Sodom and upon Gomorrah brimstone and fire from the LORD [יהוה] out of heaven." Genesis 19:24

As you can readily see in the above verse (v. 24), Moses states that the LORD who was on the earth with the two angels "rained upon Sodom and upon Gomorrah brimstone and fire from the LORD [יהוה] out of heaven." Genesis 19:24

Did you notice the little word "from" in verse 24? It says; the LORD who was on earth rained fire and brimstone "from" the Lord who was in heaven. The rain of fire and brimstone came "from" the Individual who was in heaven. And when the rain of brimstone and fire streamed through the sky, the destructive force caught the attention of the beholder and terrified the soul of its destructive power.

And when Abraham saw, from a distance, the fire and brimstone coming out of heaven upon the cities of Sodom and Gomorrah, and upon the fields, he wondered if Lot, his nephew, and his family were saved

One God or More?

from the destruction that fell upon the cities and upon the surrounding areas?

He wondered, if less than ten people were saved, or if any?

Nonetheless, as you have read in verse 24, the "LORD" who appeared to Abraham (Genesis 18:1), was the Individual who was on earth with the two angels; and He was the One who brought "brimstone and fire from the Lord out of heaven."

Since it was the LORD who interacted with Abraham on earth with the two angels, and brought "brimstone and fire" from another Individual, who was in heaven, by the name of "LORD," it means that there are two Individuals identified in v.24 by the name of "LORD." The two LORD'S are identified as two separate Individuals. One Lord [יהוה] was in heaven, and the other LORD [יהוה] was on the earth with the two angels. For that reason we can conclude that there are two Individuals mentioned in v.24, by Moses, by the name of "LORD [יהוה]."

Likewise, we have the same scenario in other verses, which reveal more than one Biblical God besides the LORD God of Israel in existence, only this time, by the name of "God."

Here is the reference, taken from the Old King James Version of the Bible (OKJV):

> "1 A Psalm of Asaph. God [אלהים] standeth in the congregation of the mighty; He judgeth among the gods."
> Psalms 82:1

And, here is the Greek text; like the Hebrew

Christ's Sovereignty.......... *By: Philip Mitanidis*

One God or More?

text, it reveals two Gods by the name of "ΘΕΟΣ [אלהים."]

> "₁ Ο ΘΕΟΣ [אלהים] Ισταται εν τη συναξει των δυνατων αναμεσον των Θεων [אלהים] θελει κρινει." Ψαλμοι 82:1 Βιβλικη Εταιρεια   Psalms 82:1

As you have noticed in the above (OKJV) of the Bible, there is only one God mentioned by the name of "אלהים" (God). And, as you have also noticed, there are many "gods" mentioned in the same verse. But, contrary to the Hebrew and to the Greek text, there is only one God of Israel mentioned instead of two in the (OKJV). That means that the verse in the (OKJV) of the Bible is mistranslated.

However, when you read the verse in the Hebrew text you will observe that there are two separate Individuals mentioned by the name of God "(אלהים;)" and that presentation in the Hebrew text and in the Greek text confirms and fortifies the fact that there are two separate Individuals mentioned by the name of God ("אלהים" "Θεων"). We are told in the Hebrew text and in the Greek text, one God stands in the midst of another God and judges the judges.

This verse refers to the time of the judges, when the LORD God of Abraham and of Israel abandoned His dwelling place in the "most holy place" of His Sanctuary, which was pitched in "Shiloh." The LORD God of Israel abandoned His Sanctuary in "Shiloh" because the children of Israel fell into apostasy. And when they fell into apostasy, the LORD God of Israel left His Sanctuary in "Shiloh" in ruins and set up, by

One God or More?

His prophets, judges to judge the children of Israel. And through the Judges, the LORD God of Abraham judged the affairs of the children of Israel.

But, time came, at one point, during the Judges, where the leaders of the children of Israel were so deeply steeped in a state of apostasy; they boldly rejected their "God" and "King" as their Judge.

Can you imagine that?

But, then again that was nothing new!

They were so bent on removing the LORD God of Israel as their "God" and "King" that they demanded from Samuel that an earthly king be set up to lead them and to judge them in all of their affairs.

After they chose Saul to be their king, Samuel anointed their choice, and in a meeting, he said to them;

> "12 And when ye [all of you] saw that Nahash the king of the children of Ammon came against you, ye said unto me, Nay; but a king shall reign over us: when the LORD your God was your King." 1 Samuel 12:12

The apostasy was so far gone that they did not even attempt to rebuild Shiloh's (the LORD God of Israel) Sanctuary, in order to continue with the ceremonial laws. They were admonished to implement the ceremonial law because it was crucial for the forgiveness of their sins. Instead, the Ark of the Covenant remained in Abinadab's house until King David brought it into Jerusalem and placed it in a tent, which he built for it. The Ark remained in the tent in anticipation of such time the Sanctuary was build for

One God or More?

the LORD God of Israel to dwell in. And the reason King David brought the Ark of the Covenant into Jerusalem was due to his love for the LORD God of his fathers; for that reason, he wanted the LORD God of Israel to reside in a stationary Temple in Jerusalem.

Nonetheless, by reading the Hebrew text and the Greek text of Psalms 82:1, a person can readily see that there are two Individuals mentioned by the name of God (אלהים Θεων) in Psalms 82:1.

Although there are many more verses that can be brought forward from the Old Testament of the Bible, which reveal and support the fact that there is more than one Individual mention by the name of God (אלהים Θεων), let me also give you a verse from the New Testament, which refers to two Individuals by the name of "LORD."

Apostle Paul writes to Timothy:

> "15 This thou [you] knowest, that all they which are in Asia be turned away from me; of whom are Phygellus and Hermogenes. 16 The Lord give mercy unto the house of Onesiphorus; for he oft refreshed me, and was not ashamed of my chain: 17 But, when he was in Rome, he sought me out very diligently, and found me.
>
>> "18 The Lord [Κυριος] grant unto him that he may find mercy of the LORD [Κυριος] in that day: and in how many things he ministered unto me at Ephesus, thou [you] knowest very well."

One God or More?

1 Timothy 1:15-18

In order to differentiate between God the Father and God the Christ, in the above verse, I have left the first word "Κυριος" (Lord), which refers to God the Father, in the lower casing; and I have made the second word "Κυριος," which refers to God the Christ, to read "LORD" in the upper casing.

Therefore, as you have noticed in the above verse, Apostle Paul desires the first Lord (God the Father), to grant unto "Onesiphorus" mercy so that "he may find mercy from the second LORD (Jesus Christ) "in that day."

The day in which Apostle Paul is making reference to is the day when Jesus Christ the LORD comes the second time to planet earth, with His holy angels, to give to every one their reward, according to their works.

> "[41] Then shall He say also unto them on the left hand, Depart from Me, ye [all of you] cursed, into everlasting fire, prepared for the devil and his angels:"
>
> "[46] And these shall go away into everlasting punishment: but the righteous into life eternal." Matthew 25:41, 46

Thus far, we have observed in the above writings of the prophets, two Individuals by the name of LORD God (God the Christ and God the Father).

In addition, I would like to bring at least one

No God Beside Me

more reference from the New Testament to show you that the apostles of Jesus Christ the LORD also identify two Individuals by the name of God (Θεος).

The verse reads as follows:

"₁ In the beginning was the Word, and the Word was with God, and the Word was God." John 1:1

It is not hard to spot the word "God" twice in the above verse (v.1). And it is not hard to understand Apostle John when he writes and identifies, in the above verse, Christ the "Word" by His name "God." And it is not incomprehensible when he writes, "the Word [Christ] was with God" to indicate that there are two separate Individuals by the name of "God" (Θεος). As you can see, there is no confusion in Apostle John's statements. He writes one God (the Word) was "with" another God.

If you are wondering why I keep referring to the word "Word" by the name of Christ, I do because Apostle John identifies the "Word" by the name of Christ by saying, "And the Word was made flesh." And then he says, the "Word" "dwelt among us"; and then he adds that the "Word" is "as of the only begotten of the Father." And then, Apostle John writes that John the Baptist "bare witness of Him [Christ the Word]."

If you want more evidence that the "Word" is Christ the LORD, read the whole chapter and draw your own conclusion.

Nonetheless, here are some of the references, which identify the "Word."

One God or More?

"₁₄ And the Word was made flesh, and dwelt among us, (and we beheld His glory, the glory as of the only begotten of the Father,) full of grace and truth.

"₁₅ John [the Baptist] bare witness of Him, and cried, saying, This was He of whom I spake, He that cometh after me is preferred before me: for He was before me." John 1:14-15

Apostle Paul sums up the above presentation that is made by Apostle John by saying,

"₁₆ And without controversy great is the mystery of godliness: God was manifest in the flesh, justified in the Spirit, seen of angels, preached unto the Gentiles, believed on in the world, received up into glory." 1 Timothy 3:16

Furthermore, in order to confirm the fact that the word "God" exists two times in John 1:1, compare the (OKJV) of the Bible with the Greek text, which reveals the fact that "God" (Christ) was with "God" (the Father) in the beginning of the creation of "all things".

"₁ In the beginning was the Word, and the Word was with God, and the Word was God." John 1:1

In confirmation that the word "God" (Θεος)

One God or More?

does exist twice in the Greek text; here is the verse in the Greek text.

"₁ Εν αρχη ητο ο Λογος, και ο Λογος ητο παρα τω Θεω, και Θεος ητο ο Λογος." Κατα Ιωαννην 1:1 Βιβλικη Εταιρεια John 1:1

To clarify the verse, it will read as follows:

"₁ Εν αρχη ητο ο Λογος [Word], και ο Λογος [Word] ητο παρα τω Θεω [God], και Θεος [God] ητο ο Λογος [Word]." Κατα Ιωαννην 1:1 Βιβλικη Εταιρεια John 1:1

    As you have read in the above verse, the word "God [Θεος]" is used twice; and as you can see, the word "God [Θεος]" does refer to God the Christ and to God the Father.
    In addition, as you have read earlier, a handful of religious institutions do not believe that Jesus Christ the LORD is "God." Therefore when they come across verses such as John 1:1, they go about throughout their lives dreaming ways as to how to get rid of verses like John 1:1, or how to delete the word "God" from these verse. And, if they can't delete the word "God" because it would be too obvious that the word is missing from the verse, as in Psalms 82:1, these religious institutions go about telling everybody that the word "God" only means a little "god" or change the verse in the Bibles, which they produce, to read in the predicate "was a god."

One God or More?

But, as hard as these religious institutions try to belittle Christ the "Word" that He is only a "little god," the verse does not allow for anyone to make the change because the Greek text in the predicate of John 1:1 reads, "and God is the Word." The Greek text emphasizes the word "God" in the predicate ("and God is the Word." "και Θεος [God] ητο ο Λογος [Word]"). The verse in the Greek text does not read "and the Word was a god."

Did you notice how badly the predicate of John 1:1 is altered by the deceivers?

Very sad don't you think to do that to Christ's holy word by men and women who call themselves Christians?

By the way, the same word "God" (Θεος) is applied to God the Father ("and the Word was with God [Θεω]"), why don't they change the word (God [Θεω]) to read there, "was a god"?

So! Why do they degrade Jesus Christ the LORD and not God the Father?

What unscriptural words will they use to defend their added, deleted, and altered words to John 1:1?

Whatever, as the saying goes, one thing will be for sure, whatever verbiage comes out of their mouths will be unholy and unscriptural and deceiving.

And at the end of any rhetoric, Scripture should be allowed to defend itself. Scripture must be allowed to interpret itself; and not some altered manufactured evil doctrine imposed upon a verse or verses of the Bible.

Therefore, we should accept what Apostle John has already written. He says, "the Word [Christ] was with God." And since the "Word" (Christ) is identified

One God or More?

by the name of "God" (Θεος), we can conclude that "God" (Θεος) the Christ was with "God" (Θεος) the Father in the beginning of the creation of "all things." And, if we accept Apostle John's presentation in John 1:1, we can readily see two Individuals mentioned by the name of "God" (Θεος).

Although I have given you a handful of verses, which reveal two Individuals by the name of "LORD" and "God," you should be made aware of the fact that the Bible mentions three separate distinct Individuals by the name of "LORD God." And that third LORD God is God the Holy Spirit who is also known by the name of the Holy Ghost.

Consequently, as per Scripture, there are three Independent Gods revealed to us; and these three Gods are as follows: God the Christ, God the Father, and God the Holy Ghost.

Here is one reference of many, which confirms the fact that there are three separate Individuals in the Godhead.

> "35 And the angel answered and said unto her [Mary], The Holy Ghost shall come upon thee [you], and the power of the Highest [God the Father] shall overshadow thee [you]: therefore also that holy thing which shall be born of thee shall be called the Son of God." Luke 1:35

Furthermore, these three Gods of the Bible are not indescribable or "unimaginable." They are real.

Although these three Gods, as per Scripture, are

One God or More?

not indescribable or "unimaginable," you will find, people still have hard time understanding who is who, especially in the Old Testament? And the reason many find it hard to understand to whom the prophets are referring to is due to the fact that they have written, most of the time, in the form of a jigsaw puzzle.

Therefore, when you read your Bible, and you find it cumbersome or hard to understand to whom the prophets of old are referring to, by the name of LORD, God, or LORD God, you should not despair.

One safe method that you can use to find out about whom the prophet of the LORD is talking about, when you come across the words "LORD" or "God," is by observing their character names. Once you learn their character names or first names if you like, you are not going to have hard time understanding about whom the prophet of the LORD is talking about.

(If you want to know Christ's character names, read my book called *"Moses Wrote About Me"* By: Philip Mitanidis.)

Here are two examples of many where Christ the LORD God of Israel uses three of His many character names —"the first and the last," "King of Israel," and "the LORD of hosts"— to identify Himself to you and to me.

Apostle John said,

"$_{17}$ And when I saw Him [Christ], I fell at His feet as dead. And He laid His right hand upon me, saying unto me, Fear not;

"I am the first and the last:

One God or More?

> "18 I am He that liveth, and was dead; and, behold, I am alive for evermore, Amen; and have the keys of hell and of death." Revelation 1:17, 18

To confirm the fact that Christ the LORD is the Individual who makes the claims that He is the LORD, the King of Israel, and the "first and the last," I am going to cross-reference the above verses with Isaiah 44:6; and please notice what "the LORD the King of Israel" said;

> "6 Thus saith the LORD the King of Israel, and his Redeemer the LORD of hosts;
>
> I am the first, and I am the last." Isaiah 44:6

As you can readily see in the above verse (v.6), Christ the "first and the last" of the (NT), Revelation 1:17, 18, is revealed in the (OT) by the same character name of "the first and the last" in Isaiah 44:6.

In addition, as you have read, Christ "the first and the last" of the New Testament (Revelation 1:17, 18) also identifies Himself in the (OT), in Isaiah 44:6, by the names of "the LORD," "King of Israel," "Redeemer," and by the name of "the LORD of hosts."

Therefore, by knowing to whom these character names belong to, you can understand the verses of the Bible much clearer. Go ahead and try it; read Isaiah, Jeremiah, Hosea, or any of the (OT) prophets, as an example, and see how clear the verses become when

One God or More?

you apply the character names of Christ to the surname of LORD, God, or LORD God.

And when you recognize to whom the character names belong to, you will be able to identify the three Individuals who go by the name of LORD and God.

Here are few examples for you to try.

"1 For, behold, the day cometh, that shall burn as an oven; and all the proud, yea, and all that do wickedly, shall be stubble: and the day that cometh shall burn them up, saith the LORD of hosts, that it shall leave them neither root nor branch. 2 But unto you that fear my name shall the Sun of righteousness arise with healing in his wings; and ye shall go forth, and grow up as calves of the stall. 3 And ye shall tread down the wicked; for they shall be ashes under the soles of your feet in the day that I shall do this, saith the LORD of hosts." Malachi 4:1-3

Who is the Individual by the name of "the LORD of hosts," from the three Gods of the Bible, which says, in Malachi 4:3, "I shall do this"?

Is He God the Father, God the Christ, or God the Holy Spirit? (Answer, it's Christ. See Revelation 1:17, 18, and compare the verse with Isaiah 44:6, and with Malachi 4:3.)

In the second example, we have the following words:

"1 In the year that King Uzziah died I saw also the LORD sitting upon a throne, high and lifted up and His train filled the temple. 2 Above it

Christ's Sovereignty.......... *By: Philip Mitanidis* 51
One God or More?

stood the seraphims: each one had six wings; with twain he covered his face, and with twain he covered his feet, and with twain he did fly. 3 And one cried unto another, and said, Holy, holy, holy, is the LORD of hosts: the whole earth is full of his glory. 4 And the posts of the door moved at the voice of him that cried, and the house was filled with smoke.

"5 Then said I, Woe is me! for I am undone; because I am a man of unclean lips, and I dwell in the midst of a people of unclean lips: for mine eyes have seen the King, the LORD of hosts." Isaiah 6:1-5

Like-wise, can you identify which one of the three Bible Gods, by the name of "the LORD of hosts" and "the King," was observed on His throne, by Isaiah, during the time when King Uzziah died?

Here are some of the references to help you identify the LORD God in Malachi 4:1-3 and in Isaiah 6:1-5.

Who is "the LORD of hosts"
in Malachi 4:1-3?

Answer: Christ. Compare Revelation 1:17, 18 with Isaiah 44:6 and then with Malachi 4:1-3.

Who is "the LORD of hosts"
in Isaiah 6:1-5

Answer: Christ. Compare Revelation 1:17, 18;

with Isaiah 44:6, and with Isaiah 6:1-5

*Who is "the King" of Israel
Mentioned in Isaiah 6:5*

Answer: Christ. Compare Isaiah 6:1-5 with Matthew 21:5; John 1:49; 19:19.

*Who did Isaiah see sitting
on His throne*

Answer: Christ. Compare Isaiah 6:1-5 with John 12:41 (Revelation 1:17, 18; Isaiah 44:6), and with the following verses.

"38 That the saying of Esaias the prophet might be fulfilled, which he spake, LORD, who hath believed our report? and to whom hath the arm of the LORD been revealed? 39 Therefore they could not believe, because that Esaias said again, 40 He hath blinded their eyes, and hardened their heart; that they should not see with their eyes, nor understand with their heart, and be converted, and I should heal them.

"41 These things said Esaias,
when he saw His [Christ's] glory,
and spake of Him.

"42 Nevertheless among the chief rulers also many believed on Him; but because of the Pharisees they did not confess Him, lest they should be put out of the synagogue" (John

Christ's Sovereignty.......... *By: Philip Mitanidis*
One God or More?

12:38-42

By using the character names of Christ the LORD of hosts, you can readily see the outcome of the above verses. They all reveal Jesus Christ the LORD by the character names of "the LORD of hosts," "the King" of Israel, sitting on His heavenly throne, and speaking prophetically of the end result of the wicked (Malachi 4:1-4).

It is easy to identify to whom the prophets of the Old Testament are referring to, when you memorize the character names of the three Gods of the Bible.

In the New Testament, you will find the same revelation of the three Gods, as you do in the (OT), only this time because the apostles and Christ the LORD have separated God the Christ, God the Father, and God the Holy Spirit from each other, by their character names, they have made it easier to observe who these three separate Individuals are.

Therefore, you can readily observe to whom the apostles are referring to when you read the New Testament of the Bible.

Furthermore, it should be noticed that God the Christ has many more character names that He goes by. Likewise, God the Father, and God the Holy Spirit also have their own character names. But, as far as their surname is concerned that surname is "LORD God," or "LORD" and "God," if you like?

Nonetheless, here are a handful of references to confirm the fact that they all have the same surname.

In reference to God the Christ's name, Moses writes:

One God or More?

"₁₄ And God said unto Moses, I AM THAT I AM: and he said, Thus shalt thou say unto the children of Israel, I AM hath sent me unto you.

"₁₅ And God said moreover unto Moses, Thus shalt thou say unto the children of Israel, The LORD God of your fathers, the God of Abraham, the God of Isaac, and the God of Jacob, hath sent me unto you: this is my name for ever, and this is my memorial unto all generations." Exodus 3:14, 15

Therefore, as it was stated earlier, the surname of the LORD GOD of Israel and of Abraham is also applied by the prophets of old to the other two Individuals of the Bible. In fact, Jesus admonishes His disciples to: "₁₉ Go ye [all of you] therefore, and teach all nations,

"baptizing them in the name of the Father, and of the Son, and of the Holy Ghost:" Matthew 28:19

Did you notice?
The above verse clearly refers to a "name"; it does not say, names.
The apostles were to baptize in the "name" of the Father, the Son, and the Holy Spirit. These three Individuals have a surname, and that name is "LORD God."
Thus in conclusion, you can readily see in the above presentation, the prophets of the LORD, all reveal more than one Biblical LORD God in existence,

One God vs. the Trinity

even though one of these three Gods, for a very good reason, makes the claim that "there is no God beside Me." And that reason is the solid fact that He is the sole Creator of "all things"; and therefore, the Sovereign LORD God of the entire creation, which He created by Himself and for Himself. See Colossians 1:16, 17 in the (OKJV), and the Greek text for confirmation.

ONE GOD vs. THE TRINITY

The fact that there are over twelve and a half thousand religious institutions out there, and each religious institution claiming that their religious doctrine is the correct one, and the other religious doctrines are in error, should cause a person's antenna to go up and realize that these religious institutions are at odds with each other. And since they do not want to give up their errors, the feud will continue to go on amongst them. But to those individuals who use the Bible to form their religious doctrine, the following verses are music to their ears, in support of their one God.

"4 Hear, O Israel: The LORD our God is one LORD: 5 And thou [you] shalt love the LORD

One God vs. the Trinity

thy [your] God with all thine [your] heart, and with all thy soul, and with all thy might" (Deuteronomy 6:4, 5).

To the relief of over two billion and a half people who use the Bible as reference to form their religious doctrines and believe that there is only one God, and to the belief of another one billion people who are lead by their priests to believe and pray to the pagan goddess Ashtar and to the god of Baal, and claim that there is one god, the above verses, and the verses in the previous chapters, which refer to one God, are welcomed by the majority of the "one God" multitude. These verses are welcomed by the one God believers because this very same multitude uses those same verses and their modern prophets to support their one God religious doctrines, and ignores the verses, which refer to the other two Gods of the Bible.

Although these groups (Jews, Muslims, and Christians) claim that there is one God, and agree in part with each other's doctrinal points, you will discover that they posture their doctrines against each other and disagree with the majority of each other's religious doctrines.

As an example, each group claims in variance that their God is the LORD God of Abraham. One group claims that the LORD God of Abraham is the "unimaginable" Supreme God of the Muslims, and not of Israel, or of the Christians.

And the majority of another group claims their Triune God, "God the Christ, God the Father, and God the Holy Spirit," is the LORD God of the Christians, and not of the Jews, or Muslims.

One God vs. the Trinity

And another group will tell you, there are three separate Individuals mentioned in the Bible by the name of "LORD God." And these three Gods exist independently from each other, think independently, act independently, have their own powers, wisdom, and might. And one of these Gods is the God of Abraham.

Therefore, you will find that there is quite a bit of posturing and antagonism going on amongst the Trinitarian believers and the "unimaginable" one God believers and the three God believers. And the reason this antagonism exists amongst these three groups is due to the fact that they all want to convert each other's followers to join their church because they each claim that the God of Abraham is with them and not with the other groups. But, since they are not conciliatory to one another, they prefer to maintain their status quo claiming that one is right and the others are wrong.

Although the above groups will continue to disagree and posture against each other's religious doctrines, it should be remembered, their goal is to convert all of the none believers to their own faith.

Therefore questions have to be asked; in reference to the LORD God of Abraham, is He one God or is He "one God in three persons"? Whose God is He? And with which groups is the LORD God of Abraham in opposition?

According to Moses, there is one God. And that God is the LORD God of Abraham, Isaac, Jacob, and of the children of Israel. He is the One who was tempted and rejected many, many times by the children of Israel, during their travels from the fields of Goshen and into the Promised Land, and in the Promised Land. He tried on numerous occasions to make the children of

One God vs. the Trinity

Israel understand that "there is no God beside Him" that they can approach, have their sins covered, make holy, be sustained, blessed, protected from Satan, and from satanic agencies.

It can readily be seen throughout the pages of the Torah, many times the children of Israel (Jacob) did not adhere to their one God of Abraham; they rejected His statutes and Commandments, and wandered far off into the dark corridors of sin, abandoned the God of their fathers, and chose to serve a multitude of pagan gods of this world (Ashtoreth, Chemoss, Milcom, Baal, etc., etc.).

But one thing is for sure, according to the following verses, there is only one Individual from the three Gods of the Bible, by the name of "LORD God," who is making the claim that there is no LORD or God beside Him that they can go to and be saved. And that claim places an exclusion upon the other two Gods of the Bible, and upon every other god that exists upon the earth and in the earth. And that exclusion means that we cannot bypass the "LORD God" of Israel and of Abraham (Exodus 20:3) and go directly to worship another LORD, God, or Lord, god, and that includes the other two Gods of the Bible.

In confirmation to His statement that there is exclusion upon all of the billions of gods that do exist, in the imaginations of men and women, the "LORD God" of Abraham and of Israel clearly states,

"$_3$ Thou [you] shalt have no other gods before Me" (Exodus 20:3).

"$_5$ I am the LORD, and there is none

One God vs. the Trinity

> else, there is no God beside Me: 6 I am the LORD, and there is none else." Isaiah 45:5, 6

As you have read, the first Commandment and the other above verses exclude the other two Gods of the Bible from receiving direct worship, and from claiming that there is no God beside them. These two excluded Gods cannot ban the LORD God of Abraham and of Israel from His Sovereign state, or place themselves in the same level as the God of Israel because He is the sole Creator, owner, and God of His creation; that is why the host of heaven worships Him.

Nehemiah declares,

> "6 Thou [You], even thou, art LORD alone; thou [You] hast made heaven, the heaven of heavens, with all their host, the earth, and all things that are therein, the seas, and all that is therein, and thou preservest them all; and the host of heaven worshippeth thee [You]" (Nehemiah 9:6).

As you have read in the above verse "the host of heaven worshippeth thee [You]." Therefore, we can conclude from the above verses that the God of Israel is referring to Himself and not to His two Associates (the other two Gods of the Bible) when He says,

> "3 Thou [you] shalt have no other gods before Me" (Exodus 20:3).

One God vs. the Trinity

> "⁵ I am the LORD, and there is none else, there is no God beside Me:" Isaiah 45:5

Moreover, you probably already have noticed in the Old Testament verses, the LORD God of Israel and of Abraham had stated more than once that there is no LORD or God beside Him. And these facts, the LORD God of Israel, not only wanted the children of Israel to know and acknowledge, but also, He wanted the inhabitants of the earth, irrespective of what religious affiliation they were involved in, to know that "there is no God beside Me." And the reason He wanted everybody to know that there is no God beside Him is due to the fact that He is the Sovereign God of all that He has created.

Therefore, worship and acknowledgement that He is the Sovereign God of "all things" goes to Him first and foremost, and not to anyone else. He cannot be bypassed. If you willfully bypass Him, He will ignore you and your prayers. And, if you do not repent and accept Him as your LORD and God, at the end, He will say to you, "I never knew you."

Here are the references:

> "²² Many will say to Me in that day, LORD, LORD, have we not prophesied in thy [Your] name? and in thy [Your] name have cast out devils? and in thy name done many wonderful works?

> "²³ And then will I profess unto them, I never knew you: depart from me, ye [all of you] that work iniquity."

One God vs. the Trinity

Matthew 7:22, 23

In order for you not to become a castaway or a reject, you should give the above verses and the first Commandment some serious thought. In fact, His first Commandment was somewhat emphatically presented to the children of Israel.

Surrounded by the host of holy angels, and standing in majesty on top of Mount Sinai, the LORD God of Israel said to the Children of Israel,

> "3 Thou [you] shalt have no other gods before Me" (Exodus 20:3).

His statement is straight forward, don't you think?

Please note, the LORD God of Israel and of Abraham said, "3 Thou [you] shalt have no other gods before Me." He said, "Me"; He did not say, before us or someone else. Therefore, grammatically, the other two Gods from the Bible, or any other gods, are not included by the use of the pronoun "Me" in the first Commandment. Consequently, His statements stand, "3 Thou [you] shalt have no other gods before Me" (Exodus 20:3).

> "5 I am the LORD, and there is none else, there is no God beside Me. 6 I am the LORD, and there is none else." Isaiah 45:5, 6

Although Scripture is clear that there is a ban placed upon worshipping directly the other two Gods of the Bible, by the God of Abraham and of Israel, the

One God vs. the Trinity

Trinitarians disagree with the Scripture references, which state, "3 Thou [you] shalt have no other gods before Me" (Exodus 20:3).

Their argument is as follows; since the Trinitarians believe in "one God in three persons," they claim that their God does not exclude the other two Gods. But contrary to their belief, there are no verses in the previous chapter or in the following verses or in the entire Bible where there are two Gods or three Gods mentioned, who unequivocally and collectively declare, suggest, or boldly state that there is no LORD or God beside Them. Therefore the exclusion stands (Exodus 20:3). As it was stated before, one of the three Gods of the Bible clearly states, "there is no God beside Me." In fact, He says, "I know not any."

In addition, the above verses are further problematic for the Trinitarians because the Trinitarians claim and believe that God the Father is the LORD God of Abraham and of Israel; and that belief, as per Scripture, is one hundred percent in error (See the next chapter for clarification.). In fact, we can include the Jews, Muslims, and some Christian institutions in the company of the Trinitarians because they all believe and teach, directly or indirectly that the God of Israel and of Abraham is God the Father. Therefore the Trinitarians say directly, it is God the Father who makes the following statements,

> "3 Thou [you] shalt have no other gods before Me" (Exodus 20:3). "5 I am the LORD, and there is none else, there is no God beside Me." Isaiah 45:5

One God vs. the Trinity

Whereby, the Jews, Muslims, and a handful of Christian churches say indirectly, it is the "unimaginable" God of Abraham who is saying, "I am the LORD and there is none else." It is claimed that their God is "unimaginable" (Translators notes page 1. Qur'an. MMP.)

Furthermore, the Trinitarians justify their beliefs that there is one God by saying there is "one God in three persons." Therefore, they claim that God the Father, God the Christ, and God the Holy Spirit are all incorporated in the above verse by the pronoun "Me," when the God of Israel says, "there is no God beside Me."

Consequently, if the Trinity is viewed as "one God" with three heads, we can ask, why is one of the three Gods claiming that there is no LORD or God beside Him?

Can He not see them?

Is He out of touch with reality?

Then again, if the Trinity is viewed as three Gods in one body, we have to conclude that they are an extension of each other; and therefore, we can also conclude, God did not die on Calvary's cross, only an extension of God died on the Cross, and therefore there was no atoning sacrifice for the sinners of planet earth.

It should also be eminent, the Trinitarian believers, like the "unimaginable" one God believers, do not have direct Scripture references to support their Trinitarian doctrine. By theorizing and explaining Scriptures way, at the end, those Bible references, which they quote to support their religious doctrine, create a big problem for the Trinitarian believers. They would have been better off, if they would have stopped

One God vs. the Trinity

and acknowledged that there are three separate independent Individuals mentioned in the Bible, instead of theorizing, and misquoting Scripture, and defending their doctrine outside of the Scriptures.

Therefore let me say again, if we accept the premise that the words "there is no God beside Me" refer to God the Father, and these words also encompass and refer to God the Christ and to God the Holy Spirit without any Scripture references to confirm those claims, we can insert, delete, and add any words or names we want in these verses to support any ideology we want to create. And, if we do, it will not make it a Scriptural fact. It would be a lie.

Furthermore, it should be noticed, these Bible verses, which state, "there is no God beside Me," also create huge problems for the Jewish believers, Muslim believers, and for a handful of Christian believers because they believe and teach their followers that there is only "one God," as in number one (1). And this LORD God, to whom they refer to, they say, he is the "unimaginable" God of Abraham and of the Torah (the five books of Moses).

As a result, since the LORD personally claims that He is the LORD God of Abraham and of Israel, you would think that the "unimaginable" one God believers, especially those religious institutions that believe only in the Old Testament, would accept the LORD God of Israel as their LORD and God. Instead, these religious institutions do not believe in many of the writings of the prophets of old, neither do they believe in Christ's words when He says to them,

"46 For had ye [all of you] believed Moses, ye

One God vs. the Trinity

would have believed Me: for he wrote of Me. 47 But if ye believe not his writings, how shall ye believe My words?" (John 5:45, 46).

In turn, they go out of their way, as far as they can, to discredit Christ and Apostle Paul and the other apostles of the New Testament who have written specifically that there is one LORD and God of the children of Israel and of Abraham.

In fact, the "unimaginable" one God believers try to discredit the Old Testament prophets who identify the LORD God of Abraham and of Israel. They also try to discredit the writings and the prophets of Christ the LORD of hosts who wrote, "there is no God beside Me." To try to discredit the LORD or His prophet's claim who wrote, "there is no God beside Me," and by not accepting the writings of the prophets of the Old Testament, and the claims Christ has made in the Old Testament, it does not help their cause and their claim that there is one indescribable and "unimaginable" God of the Old Testament because as hard as they try to defend their unscriptural stance, the more evident is the presentation of the Old Testament prophets that the God of Israel is the One who says, "there is no God beside Me."

It should also be noted; in reference to their one God, the words "unimaginable Supreme Being" are added to Scripture, these words do not appear anywhere in the Old Testament or in the New Testament of the Bible. For that reason, those uninspired words should be discarded as Scriptural proof that there is an "unimaginable Supreme Being" of the Bible.

The God of the Bible is not indescribable, or

One God vs. the Trinity

"unimaginable." There are plenty of references throughout the sixty-six books of the Bible, which clearly reveal what He looks like and who He is.

Therefore, there is no discrepancy between the Old Testament and the New Testament writings of the prophets of old. They all maintain that our God is the LORD God of Abraham and of Israel; and they also uphold the fact that He is the Individual who makes the statement that there is "no God beside Me."

As a result, the "unimaginable" God of Abraham is not the one who is making the claim in a number of Bible verses that "there is no God beside Me"; the LORD God of Israel and of Abraham is the Individual who is making that claim. In other words, the verses that are quoted by the "unimaginable" one God believers to defend their religious doctrine are verses, which refer to the LORD God of Israel. They do not refer to the indescribable and "unimaginable" one God of the Jews, Muslims, and of a handful of Christian denominations.

Consequently, if you cannot describe or identify the "unimaginable" God of Abraham, how do you know that he is indescribable or that he is the God of Abraham?

If you believe that the LORD God of Abraham and of Israel is indescribable, and "unimaginable," you are placing Him out of sight and out of mind. And when you do that, He becomes none-existent. Therefore your worship also becomes in vain because out of the billions of gods in this world, you are unable to identify your god and direct your prayers to him.

If you cannot identify with your god or God, you have to ask yourself, to whom am I praying to?

One God vs. the Trinity

On the other hand, the God of the Bible is observable, identifiable, and enteractable. He is real. Abraham saw Him face to face. Jacob saw Him "face to face" at the River Jabbok. Moses saw Him, etc., etc.

Therefore, it should be noted that none of the prophets of old acknowledge or refer to, in their writings, of an indescribable or "unimaginable" God of Abraham. There is not a single reference with those words in the entire sixty-six books of the Bible. For that reason, as I have stated before, these added, manufactured, uninspired, and unscriptural words should automatically be discarded to avoid acceptance as proof that their religious doctrine is correct.

In addition, the majority of the Jews, Muslims, and a handful of Christian institutions refuse to accept the God (God the Father) of the Greek Orthodox Church, the Protestant churches, the Roman Catholic Church, and of the Evangelical church. And the reason they do not want to accept their God, as the supreme God of Abraham, is due to the fact that these churches do not believe that "God the Father," as we know him in the New Testament, is the God of Abraham. And one reason that is sighted as to why they do not believe that "God the Father" is the God of Israel and of Abraham is due to their belief that the "one God of Abraham" "has no Son." And that statement puts the majority of the Jews, Muslims, and a handful of Christian denominations at odds with the rest of the Christian denominations because the Protestant Christian churches, the Greek Orthodox Church, and the Evangelical church believe, teach, and write in their Catechisms that "God the Father" is the God of Abraham and of Israel, and that he has a Son, and that

One God vs. the Trinity

Son is Jesus Christ.

As a result, since these Christian denominations do not believe in the indescribable, inexpressible, and "unimaginable" one God of the Jews, Muslims, and of a handful of Christian churches, and since the Muslims, Jews, and a handful of Christians do not believe in the Christian "Trinitarian doctrine," all of these religious institutions are at odds with the Bible and with each other's religious doctrinal beliefs. And, if you were to go and ask each one of these religious institutions, which uses the Bible as reference, whose religious doctrine is correct, each one will tell you that their own religious doctrine is correct and the other's religious doctrines are in error.

And to make matters even worse, you will find that there are numerous religious factions within each of these three humongous religious institutions (Jews, Muslims, and Christians), which also base their religious doctrine on the Bible. And like the church from which they evolved from, they do not agree with each other's religious doctrines. They too claim that their religious doctrine is right and everybody else's is in error.

But, how can that be?

Is there more than one Bible doctrine?

Since they all use the Bible to form their religious doctrine, shouldn't there be only one doctrine?

According to Jesus Christ the LORD and Apostle Paul, obviously there is only one Bible doctrine. Jesus Christ the LORD said,

> "14 this gospel of the kingdom shall be preached in all the world for a witness unto all nations;

One God vs. the Trinity

and then shall the end come." Matthew 24:14

Did you notice? Jesus Christ the LORD said "this gospel" shall be preached; He did not say another Gospel shall be preached. And, if another Gospel is preached, Apostle Paul warns,

> "8 But though we, or an angel from heaven, preach any other gospel unto you than that which we have preached unto you, let him be accursed.
>
> "9 As we said before, so say I now again, If any man preach any other gospel unto you than that ye [all of you] have received, let him be accursed." Galatians 1:8, 9

Very, very strong language don't you think?

Therefore, those individuals who are sincere and care about others, and about their own eternal salvation, should take heed to the apostle's warning and stop preaching another gospel than what Christ and the apostles and the prophets of the Old Testament have preached and are preaching through their written word.

If people with callous hearts or pride, harbor error, and do not want to let error go, they should take heed to Christ's statement and to Apostle Paul's warning before it is too late. I say that because there are only a handful of final prophetic sequential events remaining in the book of Revelation, which have already started and are taking place, as you are reading this page, and soon to terminate sin and unrepentant sinners who reside on planet earth and in the earth. *

One God vs. the Trinity

* (If you want detailed sequential information of the prophecy that is found in the Book of Revelation, which talks about the last events on earth, read my book called *"What is the Sign of Christ's Second Coming and the End of the World"* by Philip Mitanidis.)

Because the last prophetic events, of Revelation thirteen, are sequential events that are going to be quickly fulfilled, for the elect's sake, Apostle Paul admonishes his readers to repent and be sorry for one's sins even though repentance will bring sorrow. He writes to the Corinthian Church and admonishes the membership by saying,

> "8 For though I made you sorry with a letter, I do not repent, though I did repent: for I perceive that the same epistle hath made you sorry, though it were but for a season. 9 Now I rejoice, not that ye [all of you] were made sorry, but that ye [all of you] sorrowed to repentance: for ye [all of you] were made sorry after a godly manner, that ye might receive damage by us in nothing.

> "10 For godly sorrow worketh repentance to salvation not to be repented of: but the sorrow of the world worketh death." 2 Corinthians 6:8-10

Apostle Paul says, "godly sorrow worketh repentance," of which it brings "salvation" for the penitent sinner. For that reason Apostle Paul admonishes all the people of the world to repent and receive eternal youthful life during Christ's second

One God vs. the Trinity

coming. Apostle Paul says,

> "2 behold, now is the accepted time; behold, now is the day of salvation.).") 2 Corinthians 6:2

Do not delay repent today. Apostle Paul says, "now is the accepted time" because you do not know what tomorrow will bring your way?
But, more to the point, we do not know what the next second is going to bring our way?
Therefore, "now is the accepted time."
Remember, salvation is personal; it is between you and Jesus Christ the LORD; and it is between you and Christ because whether you know it or not, you have sinned (1 John 3:4) against Him. And in order to save you from your eternal death, He had to die on Calvary's cross for you. Therefore, let me say again, sin and salvation is personal. It is between you and Jesus Christ the LORD of hosts; no one else can save you. Without Jesus and Jesus Christ's grace, you and I will perish.
Nonetheless, going back to the "unimaginable" one God doctrine and to the three Gods doctrine (The Trinity).
Although they all claim that their church doctrine is correct, obviously sense there is only one Bible doctrine (Matthew 24:14; 2 John 9), they all cannot claim that their doctrine is correct and the rest of the religious doctrines are in error. Therefore, it should be noticed; it places the indescribable and "unimaginable" one God of Abraham believers, Jews believers, Muslims believers, and Christian believers at adds with each other's religious doctrines, with the Bible, and with the Individual who says "beside Me

One God vs. the Trinity

there is no God."

All of these religious institutions do not agree amongst each other and with the Biblical references, which state that the LORD God of Israel, the God of the Torah, and of the rest of the Old Testament writings is Christ the LORD God of Israel and of Abraham. They believe and teach contrary to the Bible, by saying that the Old Testament mostly refers to the "unimaginable" one God of Abraham and of the Torah.

On the other hand, most of the Christian churches, Greek Orthodox, Roman Catholic Church, and the majority of the Protestant churches, do not believe in the indescribable and "unimaginable" God of the Muslims. They believe contrary to Scripture that the LORD God of Abraham is "God the Father." But, as per the Torah, Christ is the LORD God of Abraham.

As a result, we have quite a doctrinal mishmash amongst these three humongous religious institutions, (Jews, Muslims, and Christians).

But, one thing is for sure, if we accept the following statements by the Individual who said, by the pen of Isaiah,

> "$_5$ I am the LORD, and there is none else, there is no God beside Me... that there is none beside Me. I am the LORD, and there is none else." Isaiah 45:5, 6,

we can at least agree with the Individual who says, "there is no God beside Me"; and we can also agree that He is the LORD God of Abraham and of the children of Israel.

What do you think at this point?

One God vs. the Trinity

Is the doctrine of the Muslim believers of the indescribable and "unimaginable" one God of Abraham" correct? Or, is the doctrine of the majority of the Christians who believe in "three Gods in one person" (The Trinity) correct? Or, is the doctrine of the believers who believe in three separate and distinct Individual Gods of the Bible correct?

So! Who is He and whose God is He?

If you said, they all don't know what they are talking about, you can add your own beliefs in the mishmash and confusion, if you sighted somebody other than Jesus Christ the LORD of hosts as the LORD God of Abraham and of Israel (Galatians 3:29).

Are you surprised?

Don't be, even though the following chapter clearly describes who He is; and identifies who, from the three Gods of the Bible, is saying,

"$_5$ I am the LORD, and there is none else, there is no God beside Me" (Isaiah 45:5),

the "unimaginable" one God believers, the Jewish believers, and the Trinitarian believers will continue to oppose each other and each other's doctrinal beliefs, stand up for their doctrine, fight to death for their doctrine, fight and die for their respective prophets, kill each other for their ideology, persecute each other, until such time, they bury their differences, and willfully migrate and join the evil agenda of the Papacy (1st beast), and of Britain and USA (2nd beast), in order to totally stamp out and extinguish the insubordinate, and the believers who believe and acknowledge Christ's Sovereignty. Although they will try to extinguish

Identifying the God of Abraham

Christ's penitent sinners, the insubordinate, Christ's Godpel, and Christ's Sovereignty from the face of the earth, Christ's words will still remain on the heavenly page, and on the printed page on earth, as a witness, which says to you and to me, as it says to Israel (Galations 3:29),

> "8 Is there a God beside Me? yea, there is no God; I know not any." Isaiah 44:8

Identifying the God of Abraham & of Israel

So, who was the Individual who went to Egypt with Moses and Aaron, took the children of Israel out of Egypt, walked with them for 40 years, and led them into the "Promised Land"? And, who is the LORD God of Abraham and of Israel? And, who is the Individual from the three Gods of the Bible claiming "there is no God beside Me"?

In order to confirm the identity of the God of Abraham and of Israel, and who claims, "there is no God beside Me," I will bring to your attention a handful of sequential events from the Torah (the five books of Moses) for your consideration. The overview of the Torah will not only help us to identify the LORD God of Abraham and of Israel, at the same time, it will give us a glimpse of the children of Israel, of their journey to

Identifying the God of Abraham

the Promised Land, and of their attitude towards the God of their fathers, Moses, and Aaron, during their wandering in the deserts between the Negeb and Egypt.

As you probably already know, Moses was born of Hebrew blood; and more precisely of Levitical blood, spent most of his time, during his forty youthful years, in Egypt, in the courts of Pharaoh. There Moses was diligently prepped for the throne of Pharaoh. For that reason, he was tutored in the sciences, self-defense, combat, architecture, languages, countries, warfare, enemies of Egypt, royalty, etc., etc. But, in his mother's arms, Moses was also tutored in the ways of the God of Abraham and of Israel.

One day when Moses was forty years old, he decided to go out and mingle with the slaves in order to find out first hand why they were complaining about their work conditions.

The record states:

> "11 And it came to pass in those days, when Moses was grown, that he went out unto his brethren, and looked on their burdens: and he spied an Egyptian smiting an Hebrew, one of his brethren. 12 And he looked this way and that way, and when he saw that there was no man, he slew the Egyptian, and hid him in the sand.

> "13 And when he went out the second day, behold, two men of the Hebrews strove together: and he said to him that did the wrong, Wherefore smitest thou [you] thy [your] fellow? 14 And he said, Who made thee [you] a prince and a judge over us? intendest thou [you] to kill

me, as thou [you] killedst the Egyptian? And Moses feared, and said, Surely this thing is known.

"15 Now when Pharaoh heard this thing, he sought to slay Moses. But Moses fled from the face of Pharaoh, and dwelt in the land of Midian: and he sat down by a well.

"16 Now the priest of Midian had seven daughters: and they came and drew water, and filled the troughs to water their father's flock. 17 And the shepherds came and drove them away: but Moses stood up and helped them, and watered their flock. 18 And when they came to Reuel their father, he said, How is it that ye [all of you] are come so soon to day?

"19 And they said, An Egyptian delivered us out of the hand of the shepherds, and also drew water enough for us, and watered the flock. 20 And he said unto his daughters, And where is he? why is it that ye [all of you] have left the man? call him, that he may eat bread.

"21 And Moses was content to dwell with the man: and he gave Moses Zipporah his daughter. 22 And she bare him a son, and he called his name Gershom: for he said, I have been a stranger in a strange land.

"23 And it came to pass in process of time, that the king of Egypt died: and the children of Israel

Identifying the God of Abraham

sighed by reason of the bondage, and they cried, and their cry came up unto God by reason of the bondage. 24 And God heard their groaning, and God remembered His covenant with Abraham, with Isaac, and with Jacob. 25 And God looked upon the children of Israel, and God had respect unto them.

"1 Now Moses kept the flock of Jethro his father in law, the priest of Midian: and he led the flock to the backside of the desert, and came to the mountain of God, even to Horeb. 2 And the angel of the LORD appeared unto him in a flame of fire out of the midst of a bush: and he looked, and, behold, the bush burned with fire, and the bush was not consumed. 3 And Moses said, I will now turn aside, and see this great sight, why the bush is not burnt. 4 And when the LORD saw that he turned aside to see, God called unto him out of the midst of the bush, and said, Moses, Moses. And he said, Here am I. 5 And He said, Draw not nigh hither: put off thy [your] shoes from off thy [your] feet, for the place whereon thou [you] standest is holy ground.

"6 Moreover He said, I am the God of thy [your] father, the God of Abraham, the God of Isaac, and the God of Jacob. And Moses hid his face; for he was afraid to look upon God.

Christ's Sovereignty……... *By: Philip Mitanidis*
Identifying the God of Abraham

"₇ And the LORD said, I have surely seen the affliction of My people which are in Egypt, and have heard their cry by reason of their taskmasters; for I know their sorrows;

"₈ And I am come down to deliver them out of the hand of the Egyptians,

"and to bring them up out of that land unto a good land and a large, unto a land flowing with milk and honey; unto the place of the Canaanites, and the Hittites, and the Amorites, and the Perizzites, and the Hivites, and the Jebusites. ₉ Now therefore, behold, the cry of the children of Israel is come unto Me: and I have also seen the oppression wherewith the Egyptians oppress them.

"₁₀ Come now therefore, and I will send thee [you] unto Pharaoh, that thou [you] mayest bring forth My people the children of Israel out of Egypt."
Exodus 2:11-25; 3:1-10

As you have read, forty years later, when Moses was eighty years old, the God of Abraham, Isaac, Jacob, and of the children of Israel (Exodus 3:14, 15) appeared unto Moses near Mount Sinai; and said to Moses that He has "come down" on earth (Exodus 3:8) to go with Moses to Egypt, according to verse (v.10), to take His people, the children of Israel, to the Promised

Identifying the God of Abraham

Land.

But, why was The God of Abraham and of Israel (Jacob) going to take the children of Israel out of Egypt?

He was going to take them out of Egypt because He had promised Abraham that He would eventually take his descendants out of Egypt and give them the land Abraham was standing on.

The intent of the LORD God of Abraham and of Israel was well and good; but Moses felt intimidated by God's recommendation. He was intimidated because Moses for the past forty years was out of touch with the outside world; day in and day out, he was out in the dessert looking after the animals. He had no one there to talk to, to keep him company, or to interact with. Therefore because he did not have many people to interact with during his forty years in the desert, or being involved in projects whereby he kept up with all of the subjects in the arts, warfare, sciences, etc., etc., to keep his mind advancing in knowledge and understanding, he became slow to speak. In fact, Moses said to the LORD,

> "10 O my LORD, I am not eloquent, neither heretofore, nor since thou [You] hast spoken unto thy [Your] servant: but I am slow of speech, and of a slow tongue." Exodus 4:10

Moses acknowledged his inadequacies. He had forgotten most of the things he had leaned in the courts of Pharaoh. He could not talk eloquently, he did not

Identifying the God of Abraham

know what the current customs were when appearing before dignitaries, he did not know what to say when he appeared before Pharaoh, he also did not know what to say to the elders of the children of Israel, etc., etc.

In encouragement,

> "11 the LORD said unto him, Who hath made man's mouth? or who maketh the dumb, or deaf, or the seeing, or the blind? have not I the LORD? 12 Now therefore go, and I will be with thy [your] mouth, and teach thee [you] what thou [you] shalt say." Exodus 4:11

Moses consented to go to Egypt after the LORD God of Abraham and of Israel said to Moses that He would be with him; and the LORD also promised to send his older brother Aaron from Egypt to meet him and accept him as his helper. And after they meet, all three of them were to make the journey to Egypt together. And when they arrive there, they were to go to the elders of the children of Israel and tell them that they are on a mission sent by the LORD God of their fathers. And that mission is to take the children of Israel out of Egypt and into the Promised Land.

After many questions posed by the elders of Israel, they chose to accept Aaron and Moses as the messengers of God. Therefore, shortly after, Moses and Aaron went to Pharaoh and asked him to let the children of Israel leave Egypt. Pharaoh considered the request ridiculous; and said to Moses and Aaron, who is this God that I should obey Him? Therefore he adamantly refused to let the children of Israel leave Egypt. But, after a number of plagues that were cast

Identifying the God of Abraham

upon Egypt, and the last plague, which killed all of the first-born animals and all of the first-born children in Egypt, Pharaoh,

> "28 said unto him [Moses], Get thee [you] from me, take heed to thyself, see my face no more; for in that day thou [you] seest my face thou shalt die.
>
> "29 And Moses said, Thou [you] hast spoken well, I will see thy [your] face again no more." Exodus 10:28, 29

"29 And it came to pass, that at midnight the LORD smote all the firstborn in the land of Egypt, from the firstborn of Pharaoh that sat on his throne unto the firstborn of the captive that was in the dungeon; and all the firstborn of cattle.
"30 And Pharaoh rose up in the night, he, and all his servants, and all the Egyptians; and there was a great cry in Egypt; for there was not a house where there was not one dead. 31 And he called for Moses and Aaron by night, and said, Rise up, and get you forth from among my people, both ye and the children of Israel; and go, serve the LORD, as ye have said." Exodus." 12:29-31
"35 And the children of Israel did according to the word of Moses; and they borrowed of the Egyptians jewels of silver, and jewels of gold, and raiment: 36 And the LORD gave the people favour in the sight of the Egyptians, so that they lent unto them such things as they required. And they spoiled the Egyptians. 37 And the children of Israel journeyed from Raamses to

Identifying the God of Abraham

Succoth, about six hundred thousand on foot that were men, beside children. 38 And a mixed multitude went up also with them; and flocks, and herds, even very much cattle." Exodus 12:35-38

According to 1 Kings 6:1, the children of Israel (Jacob) left Egypt from the fields of Goshen, around 1445 BC. From there, they were lead by a cloud by the God of Abraham to a place called "Succoth" (Genesis 12:37). Moses wrote:

> "21 And the LORD went before them by day in a pillar of a cloud, to lead them the way; and by night in a pillar of fire, to give them light; to go by day and night:
>
> "22 He took not away the pillar of the cloud by day, nor the pillar of fire by night, from before the people." Exodus 13:21, 22

Now that we have an introduction to the Torah, to the children of Israel, to the LORD God of Abraham, and to Israel, we can ask,

Who is this LORD God of Abraham and of Israel who went to Egypt with Moses and Aaron and led the children of Israel out of Egypt in a cloud?

Previously, if you recall, although the verses from the Torah clearly reveal that the God of Abraham

Identifying the God of Abraham

is the God of Isaac, the God of Jacob (Israel), and the God of the children of Israel, all of the religious denominations that I know of, which use the Bible to form their religious doctrine, do not agree with each other as to who is the God of Abraham and of Israel?

As an example, as it was revealed previously, the Jews, Muslims, and a handful of Christian denominations believe that the God of Abraham, Isaac, Jacob, and of the children of Israel is the God who took the children of Israel out of Egypt, divided the Red Sea, and gave them the land of Canaan as their inheritance. And that God, they say, is "the unimaginable God of Abraham."

Since that is their belief and their God is "inconceivable" that means that they have no clue who is the God of Abraham.

As per their own statement, they cannot identify Him!

On the other hand, given that the majority of the Christian denominations (Protestant churches, Greek Orthodox Church, and Roman Catholic Church), believe that the God of Abraham, and of the children of Israel is "God the Father," can they be believed that God the Father is the God of Abraham and of Israel?

Can their belief be a Biblical fact? After all, over three billion people cannot be wrong?

Can they?

Of course they can!

Therefore, if you find the following presentation by Apostle Paul disturbing, and contrary to your belief, you should thank the LORD God of Abraham, and of the children of Israel for His revelation, and for men like Apostle Paul who stood up for the truth under the

Identifying the God of Abraham

threats of beatings, hunger, imprisonment, all manner of persecution, oppression, and even death.

Although you and I might or might not go through the severe persecution Apostle Paul and the rest of the prophets of the LORD went through, for preaching His word, shouldn't we, all the more, stand up for the Gospel truth and do likewise?

If we love Christ the LORD for what He did for us on Calvary's cross, obviously, we will. And, if we don't, it reveals our hateful callous character towards Christ the LORD of hosts and towards His penitent sinners and towards His Gospel. For those reasons, we will stand up for the truth or for error.

Nonetheless, whatever our choice, let us consider few Biblical references and see, if the beliefs of the above three humongous religious denominations are correct or not?

Therefore, to identify who is the God of Abraham, and of the children of Israel, and to reveal who went to Egypt with Moses and with his older brother Aaron, led the children of Israel out of Egypt, fed them, gave them water to drink from rocks, sustained them, protected them, and gave them the Promise Land, I would like to cross-reference the verses from the Torah, with the verses that are found in the New Testament (Greek text), and see who is the Individual that identifies Himself by the name of the LORD God of Abraham, and of the children of Israel?

Therefore let me first ask you, who led the children of Israel by a cloud out of Egypt from the fields of Raamses, was it God the Christ, was it God the Father, or was

Identifying the God of Abraham

somebody else involved with the children of Israel?

From the fields of Rameses.

Moses wrote:

"17 And it came to pass, when Pharaoh had let the people go, that God led them not through the way of the land of the Philistines, although that was near; for God said, Lest peradventure the people repent when they see war, and they return to Egypt: 18 But God led the people about, through the way of the wilderness of the Red sea: and the children of Israel went up harnessed out of the land of Egypt.

"19 And Moses took the bones of Joseph with him: for he had straitly sworn the children of Israel, saying, God will surely visit you; and ye shall carry up my bones away hence with you.

"20 And they took their journey from Succoth, and encamped in Etham, in the edge of the wilderness.

> "21 And the LORD went before them by day in a pillar of a cloud, to lead them the way; and by night in a pillar of fire, to give them light; to go by day and night: 22 He took not away the pillar of the cloud by day, nor the

Identifying the God of Abraham

pillar of fire by night, from before the people." Exodus 13:17-22

So! Who was the Individual that led the children of Israel by a cloud from the fields of Rameses and all the way into the Promised Land?
Here is Apostle Paul's answer.
Apostle Paul wrote:

* "1 MOREOVER, brethren, I would not that ye [all of you] should be ignorant, how that all our fathers *[the children of Israel] were under the cloud,* and all passed though the sea;

* "2 And were all baptized unto Moses *in the cloud* and in the sea;

"3 And did all eat the same spiritual meat;

* "4 And did all drink the same spiritual drink: for they drank of that spiritual Rock that followed them: and that Rock was *Christ* [Χριστος]" (1 Corinthians 10:1-4).

And, here are the cross-references in the Greek text, which confirm the fact that the word Christ (Χριστος) does exist in verse four of Corinthians 10 to let us know that it was Jesus Christ the LORD God of Abraham and of the children of Israel who interacted with the children of Israel and led them in a cloud all the way into the Promised Land.

Identifying the God of Abraham

* "1 ΔΕΝ θελω δε να αγνοητε, αδελφοι, οτι οι πατερες ημων ησαν παντες υπο *την νεφελην*, και παντες δια της θαλασσης διηλθον

* "2 και παντες εις τον Μωυσην εβαπτισθησαν *εν τη νεφελη* και εν τη θαλασση

"3 και παντες την αυτην πνευματικην βρωσιν εφαγον

* "4 και παντες το αυτο πνευματικον ποτον επιον διοτι επινον απο πνευματικης πετρας ακολουθουσης η δε πετρα ητο ο *Χριστος* [Christ]." Προς Κορινθιους Α' 10:1-4 Βιβλικη Εταιρεια 1 Corinthians 10:1-4

As you can readily see in the above verses (1, 2, 4) of the OKJV of the Bible, and in the Greek text, Apostle Paul points out that the Individual who led the children of Israel out of Egypt by a cloud was none other than Jesus "Christ [Χριστος]" (v.4).

Consequently, according to Apostle Paul, Jesus Christ is the LORD God of Abraham and of the children of Israel.

Are you surprised?

Don't be! Here is further evidence, which identifies Jesus Christ, as we know Him now in the New Testament, interacting with the children of Israel and accepting Him as their LORD and God.

As per the Torah, the cloud led the children of Israel southwest from the fields of Rameses to a place called "Sucoth." And from Succoth they traveled to a place called "Etham" (Exodus 13:20). And from Etham

Identifying the God of Abraham

the children of Israel journeyed and camped between Migdol and the Red Sea (Gulf of Suez).

Therefore, we can ask, who was the Individual who led the children of Israel by a cloud out of Egypt, and told them to camp between Migdol and the Red Sea?

Between Migdol and the Red Sea.

Here are the events, which took place between Migdol and the Red Sea; and the answer as to who delivered the children of Israel from the enraged hand of Pharaoh?

"1 And the LORD spake unto Moses, saying, 2 Speak unto the children of Israel, that they turn and encamp before Pihahiroth, between Migdol and the sea, over against Baalzephon: before it shall ye encamp by the sea." Exodus 14:1, 2

And when Pharaoh heard where the children of Israel were camped, and they had no way of escape, if they were to be attacked, vindictively he saw an opportunity to go and annihilate the children of Israel from the face of the earth.

Pharaoh, quickly mounted his chariot, and when his army mounted their 600 chariots, they followed him to Israel's campsite. And when the children of Israel saw the Egyptian army coming towards them, and the rumble of the wheals of the chariots were heard, they panicked and fear struck the whole camp of Israel. But

Identifying the God of Abraham

Moses stood before them and told them not to fear because the LORD God of Israel would fight for them, and help them to escape their ferocious oppressive foe.

Here are the references taken from the Torah (the five books of Moses) when the LORD God of Israel divided the Red Sea and made an escape for the children of Israel and prevented an onslaught by the hateful hand of Pharaoh's army.

> "21 And Moses stretched out his hand over the sea; and the LORD caused the sea to go back by a strong east wind all that night, and made the sea dry land, and the waters were divided.
>
> "22 And the children of Israel went into the midst of the sea upon the dry ground: and the waters were a wall unto them on their right hand, and on their left.
>
> "23 And the Egyptians pursued, and went in after them to the midst of the sea, even all Pharaoh's horses, his chariots, and his horsemen.
>
> "24 And it came to pass, that in the morning watch the LORD looked unto the host of the Egyptians through the pillar of fire and of the cloud, and troubled the host of the Egyptians, 25 And took off their chariot wheels, that they drave them heavily: so that the Egyptians said, Let us flee from the face of Israel; for the LORD fighteth for them against the Egyptians.
>
> "26 And the LORD said unto Moses, Stretch out thine [your] hand over the sea, that the waters may come again upon the Egyptians, upon their chariots, and

Identifying the God of Abraham

upon their horsemen. 27 And Moses stretched forth his hand over the sea, and the sea returned to his strength when the morning appeared; and the Egyptians fled against it; and the LORD overthrew the Egyptians in the midst of the sea.

"28 And the waters returned, and covered the chariots, and the horsemen, and all the host of Pharaoh that came into the sea after them; there remained not so much as one of them.

"29 But the children of Israel walked upon dry land in the midst of the sea; and the waters were a wall unto them on their right hand, and on their left.

"30 Thus the LORD saved Israel that day out of the hand of the Egyptians; and Israel saw the Egyptians dead upon the sea shore. 31 And Israel saw that great work which the LORD did upon the Egyptians: and the people feared the LORD, and believed the LORD, and His servant Moses." Exodus 14:21-31

Therefore, as per the above verses, the LORD God of Abraham and of Israel is the One who blinded Pharaoh and his army so that they were not able to see where they were going. Then He set a blazing fire before Pharaoh's army so that the children of Israel were able to see where they were going, divided the Red Sea, allowed safe dry passage to the children of Israel through the Red Sea to cross to the other side of the sea. Then He removed the gross darkness from Pharaoh and from his army so that they were able to see their surroundings. And when they did, Pharaoh gave the order to pursue the children of Israel through the dry passage that was carved in the sea. The LORD God of Israel allowed Pharaoh's army to pursue the children of Israel into the Red Sea, and just before Pharaoh's army

Identifying the God of Abraham

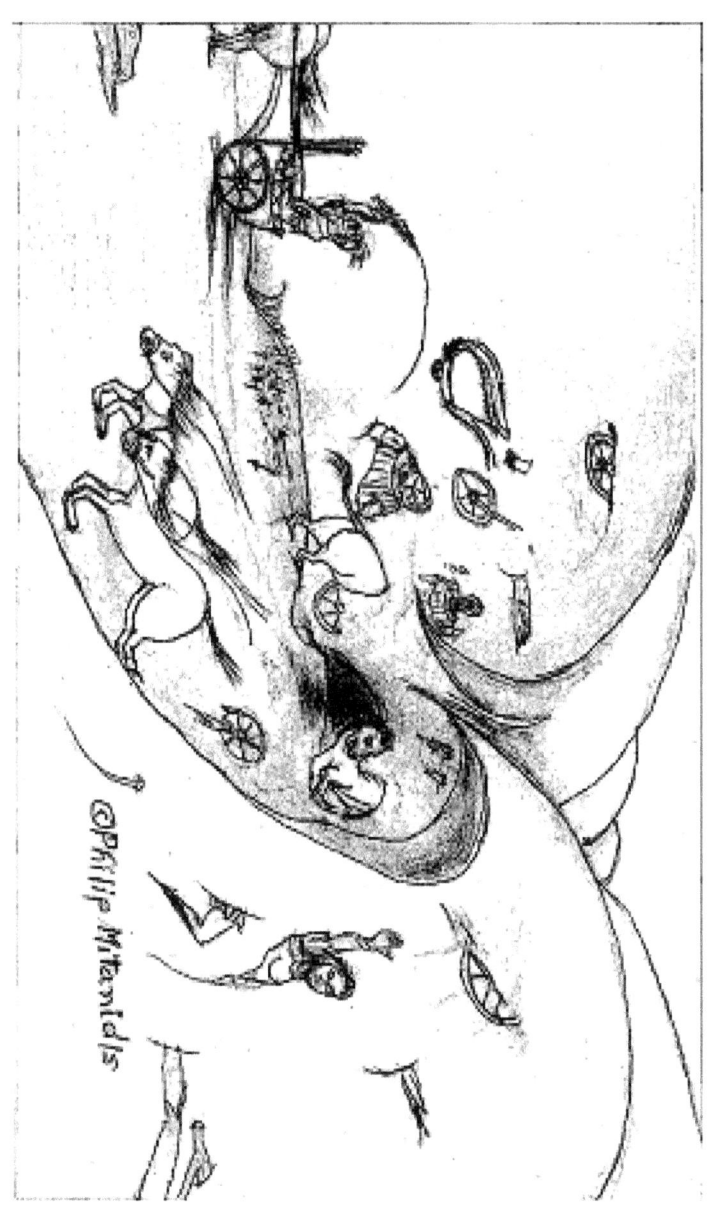

Identifying the God of Abraham

reached the other side of the Sea, Moses raised his arms, and the LORD, the God of Israel, covered the passage with water and drowned the horses, the chariots, and its riders. The LORD God of Israel, better known to the children of Israel as the LORD God of Abraham was the Individual who "divided the sea" for the children of Israel.

Did you notice; it was the "LORD God of Abraham and of Israel who said to Moses to stretch his hand over the sea,

> "$_{21}$ And Moses stretched out his hand over the sea; and the LORD caused the sea to go back by a strong east wind all that night, and made the sea dry land, and the waters were divided.

> "$_{22}$ And the children of Israel went into the midst of the sea upon the dry ground: and the waters were a wall unto them on their right hand, and on their left." Exodus 14:21, 22

So, who is this LORD God of Israel of whom Moses is referring to? Who "divided" the sea (v.21), and made a safe passage for the children of Israel to cross over the other side of the sea?

Here is the answer given to us by Apostle Paul in regards to the Individual that is mentioned by the name of "LORD" in the above verses (Exodus 14:21-31).

Apostle Paul wrote,

Identifying the God of Abraham

* "₁ MOREOVER, brethren, I would not that ye [all of you] should be ignorant, how that all our fathers [the children of Israel] were under the cloud, and *all passed though the sea;*

* "₂ And were all baptized unto Moses in the cloud and *in the sea;*

  "₃ And did all eat the same spiritual meat;

* "₄ And did all drink the same spiritual drink: for they drank of that spiritual Rock that followed them: and that Rock was *Christ* [Χριστος]" (1 Corinthians 10:1-4).

Here are the cross-references in the Greek text, which confirm the facts that the word Christ (Χριστος) does exist in verse four of Corinthians 10 to let us know that it was Jesus Christ the LORD God of Abraham and of the children of Israel who interacted with the children of Israel and delivered them from Pharaoh's army.

The Greek text reads:

* "₁ ΔΕΝ θελω δε να αγνοητε, αδελφοι, οτι οι πατερες ημων ησαν παντες υπο την νεφελην, και παντες *δια της θαλασσης διηλθον*

* "₂ και παντες εις τον Μωυσην εβαπτισθησαν εν τη νεφελη και *εν τη θαλασση*

  "₃ και παντες την αυτην πνευματικην βρωσιν εφαγον

Christ's Sovereignty......... By: Philip Mitanidis
Identifying the God of Abraham

* "4 και παντες το αυτο πνευματικον ποτον επιον διοτι επινον απο πνευματικης πετρας ακολουθουσης η δε πετρα ητο ο *Χριστος* [Christ]." Προς Κορινθιους Α' 10:1-4 Βιβλικη Εταιρεια 1 Corinthians 10:1-4

And when you consider verses one, two, and four of 1 Corinthians 10, you will notice in the (OKJV) of the Bible and in the Greek text, they both confirm the fact that the Individual who led the children of Israel in a "cloud" from the fields of Raamses, and "divided the sea," "and all passed through the sea" ("και παντες δια της θαλασσης διηλθον") v.1, was none other than "Christ" (Χριστος) 1 Corinthians 10:4.

Therefore, according to Apostle Paul, since it was Christ (Χριστος) who led the children of Israel in a "cloud," and "divided the sea," it follows as per Exodus 14:21, 22, and 1 Corinthians 10:1, 2, 4, it was Christ (Χριστος) the LORD God of Israel who "divided the sea," and all passed through the sea ("και παντες δια της θαλασσης διηλθον") v.1, to let the children of Israel escape the mighty arm of Pharaoh.

Let me say again, since it was the LORD God of Israel who claimed that He divided the Red Sea and made a dry passage for the children of Israel to pass safely to the other side of the sea, Apostle Paul confirms that event in verses one and two of 1 Corinthians 10, and identifies the LORD God of Abraham and of Israel by the name of "Christ" (Χριστος) in 1 Corinthians 10:4.

Therefore, the LORD God of Israel, who led the children of Israel in a "cloud" and "divided the sea," according to Apostle Paul (1 Corinthians 10:1, 2, 4), is

Identifying the God of Abraham

identified in the above verses by the character name of "Christ" (Χριστος).

As a result, according to Apostle Paul, Christ is the LORD God of Israel, who said to Moses; stretch your hand over the sea,

> "21 And Moses stretched out his hand over the sea; and the LORD caused the sea to go back by a strong east wind all that night, and made the sea dry land, and the waters were divided." Exodus 14:21

And when Pharaoh's army followed the children of Israel in pursuit in the dry passage, Moses was asked to raise his hand over the passage, "28 And the waters returned, and covered the chariots, and the horsemen, and all the host of Pharaoh that came into the sea after them; there remained not so much as one of them." Exodus 14:28

"20 And Miriam the prophetess, the sister of Aaron, took a timbrel in her hand; and all the women went out after her with timbrels and with dances. 21 And Miriam answered them, Sing ye [all of you] to the LORD, for He hath triumphed gloriously; the horse and his rider hath He thrown into the sea" (Exodus 15:20, 21).

Therefore we can conclude, as per the above presentation, according to Apostle Paul, it was Christ (Χριστος) the LORD God of Abraham and of Israel who drowned the horse and its rider into the Red Sea (Exodus 14:27; 1 Corinthians 10:1, 2, 4).

Identifying the God of Abraham

The children of Israel tempted the LORD God of Israel in the Wilderness of Shur.

After "22 Moses brought Israel from the Red sea," "they went out into the wilderness of Shur; and they went three days in the wilderness, and found no water. 23 And when they came to Marah, they could not drink of the waters of Marah, for they were bitter: therefore the name of it was called Marah.
"24 And the people murmured against Moses, saying, What shall we drink?
"25 And he cried unto the LORD; and the LORD shewed him a tree, which when he had cast into the waters, the waters were made sweet: there he made for them a statute and an ordinance, and there he proved them,

> "26 And said, If thou [you] wilt diligently hearken to the voice of the LORD thy [your] God, and wilt do that which is right in His sight, and wilt give ear to His commandments, and keep all His statutes, I will put none of these diseases upon thee, which I have brought upon the Egyptians: for I am the LORD that healeth thee [you].

"27 And they came to Elim, where were twelve wells of water, and threescore and ten palm trees: and they encamped there by the waters." Exodus 15:20-27

Tempting the LORD in the Wilderness of Sin

"1 And they took their journey from Elim, and

Identifying the God of Abraham

all the congregation of the children of Israel came unto the wilderness of Sin, which is between Elim and Sinai, on the fifteenth day of the second month after their departing out of the land of Egypt.

"2 And the whole congregation of the children of Israel murmured against Moses and Aaron in the wilderness:

> "3 And the children of Israel said unto them, Would to God we had died by the hand of the LORD in the land of Egypt, when we sat by the flesh pots, and when we did eat bread to the full; for ye [all of you] have brought us forth into this wilderness, to kill this whole assembly with hunger.

"4 Then said the LORD unto Moses, Behold, I will rain bread from heaven for you; and the people shall go out and gather a certain rate every day, that I may prove them, whether they will walk in My law, or no. 5 And it shall come to pass, that on the sixth day they shall prepare that which they bring in; and it shall be twice as much as they gather daily.

"6 And Moses and Aaron said unto all the children of Israel, At even, then ye [all of you] shall know that the LORD hath brought you out from the land of Egypt: 7 And in the morning, then ye shall see the glory of the LORD; for that He heareth your murmurings against the LORD: and what are we, that ye [all of you] murmur against us?

"8 And Moses said, This shall be, when the LORD shall give you in the evening flesh to eat, and in

Identifying the God of Abraham

the morning bread to the full; for that the LORD heareth your murmurings which ye murmur against Him: and what are we? your murmurings are not against us, but against the LORD. 9 And Moses spake unto Aaron, Say unto all the congregation of the children of Israel, Come near before the LORD: for He hath heard your murmurings.

"10 And it came to pass, as Aaron spake unto the whole congregation of the children of Israel, that they looked toward the wilderness, and, behold, the glory of the LORD appeared in the cloud. 11 And the LORD spake unto Moses, saying, 12 I have heard the murmurings of the children of Israel: speak unto them, saying, At even ye shall eat flesh, and in the morning ye shall be filled with bread; and ye shall know that I am the LORD your God.

"13 And it came to pass, that at even the quails came up, and covered the camp: and in the morning the dew lay round about the host. 14 And when the dew that lay was gone up, behold, upon the face of the wilderness there lay a small round thing, as small as the hoar frost on the ground. 15 And when the children of Israel saw it, they said one to another, It is manna: for they wist not what it was. And Moses said unto them, This is the bread which the LORD hath given you to eat. 16 This is the thing which the LORD hath commanded, Gather of it every man according to his eating, an omer for every man, according to the number of your persons; take ye every man for them which are in his tents.

"17 And the children of Israel did so, and gathered, some more, some less. 18 And when they did mete it with an omer, he that gathered much had

Identifying the God of Abraham

nothing over, and he that gathered little had no lack; they gathered every man according to his eating. 19 And Moses said, Let no man leave of it till the morning. 20 Notwithstanding they hearkened not unto Moses; but some of them left of it until the morning, and it bred worms, and stank: and Moses was wroth with them.

"21 And they gathered it every morning, every man according to his eating: and when the sun waxed hot, it melted. 22 And it came to pass, that on the sixth day they gathered twice as much bread, two omers for one man: and all the rulers of the congregation came and told Moses. 23 And he said unto them, This is that which the LORD hath said, To morrow is the rest of the holy sabbath unto the LORD: bake that which ye will bake to day, and seethe that ye will seethe; and that which remaineth over lay up for you to be kept until the morning.

"24 And they laid it up till the morning, as Moses bade: and it did not stink, neither was there any worm therein. 25 And Moses said, Eat that to day; for to day is a sabbath unto the LORD: to day ye shall not find it in the field. 26 Six days ye shall gather it; but on the seventh day, which is the sabbath, in it there shall be none.

"27 And it came to pass, that there went out some of the people on the seventh day for to gather, and they found none. 28 And the LORD said unto Moses, How long refuse ye [all of you] to keep My commandments and My laws? 29 See, for that the LORD hath given you the sabbath, therefore He giveth you on the sixth day the bread of two days; abide ye every man in his place, let no man go out of his place on the seventh day. 30 So the people rested on the

Identifying the God of Abraham

seventh day.

"31 And the house of Israel called the name thereof Manna: and it was like coriander seed, white; and the taste of it was like wafers made with honey. 32 And Moses said, This is the thing which the LORD commandeth, Fill an omer of it to be kept for your generations; that they may see the bread wherewith I have fed you in the wilderness, when I brought you forth from the land of Egypt.

"33 And Moses said unto Aaron, Take a pot, and put an omer full of manna therein, and lay it up before the LORD, to be kept for your generations. 34 As the LORD commanded Moses, so Aaron laid it up before the Testimony, to be kept. 35 And the children of Israel did eat manna forty years, until they came to a land inhabited; they did eat manna, until they came unto the borders of the land of Canaan." Exodus 16:1-35

So! Who is the Individual that "divided the sea," led the children of Israel in a cloud to the Wilderness of Sin, fed them quails, and bread (manna) to eat?

According to the above verses, He is "the God of Israel." In fact in v.11 above, He even claimed to the children of Israel, "I am the LORD your God." And this very same LORD God is further identified by His character name of "Christ" (Χριστος) by Apostle Paul in 1 Corinthians 10:4.

Apostle Paul writes,

"1 MOREOVER, brethren, I would not that ye should be ignorant, how that all our fathers [the

Identifying the God of Abraham

children of Israel] were under the cloud, and all passed though the sea;

"2 And were all baptized unto Moses in the cloud and in the sea;

* "**3** *And did all eat the same spiritual meat [food];*

* "**4** And did all drink the same spiritual drink: for they drank of that spiritual Rock that followed them: and that Rock was *Christ* [Χριστος]" (1 Corinthians 10:1-4).

And here are the above verses in the Greek text, which confirm the facts in v.4 that it was "Christ" (Χριστος) who "divided the sea," ("και παντες δια της θαλασσης διηλθον") to let the children of Israel escape, through the divided sea, the mighty arm of Pharaoh, led them by a cloud to the Wilderness of Shur; and later He led them into the Wilderness of Sin, fed them quails and manna to eat "3 και παντες την αυτην πνευματικην βρωσιν εφαγον" (v.3).

Here are the verses in the Greek text:

"1 ΔΕΝ θελω δε να αγνοητε, αδελφοι, οτι οι πατερες ημων ησαν παντες υπο την νεφελην, και παντες δια της θαλασσης διηλθον

"2 και παντες εις τον Μωυσην εβαπτισθησαν εν τη νεφελη και εν τη θαλασση

* "**3** *και παντες την αυτην πνευματικην βρωσιν*

Identifying the God of Abraham

εφαγον

* "4 και παντες το αυτο πνευματικον ποτον επιον διοτι επινον απο πνευματικης πετρας ακολουθουσης η δε πετρα ητο ο *Χριστος* [Christ]." Προς Κορινθιους Α' 10:1-4   Βιβλικη Εταιρεια 1 Corinthians 10:1-4

Therefore as per the above verses, it was "Christ" the "God of Israel" who gave them meat and bread to eat in the Wilderness of Sin. And again, according to Apostle Paul in 1 Corinthians 10:3, and 4, the Individual who led them in a "cloud" and fed the children of Israel quails and manna, was none other than Christ ("Χριστος") the "LORD God of Israel."

Tempting the LORD at Rephidim.

After the children of Israel rested in the "Wilderness of Sin," Christ the LORD God of Israel led the children of Israel and their animals to a place called "Rephidim" (Exodus 17:1), which is closer to Mount Sinai. And there the children of Israel and their animals ran out of water, and therefore they thirsted. And since there was no water to be seen anywhere in the area, the children of Israel began to be unruly and ready to stone Moses and Aaron.

And while the children of Israel were camped at Rephidim," Moses describes the mood of the people against Aaron and himself; he writes, "2 Wherefore the people did chide with Moses, and said, Give us water that we may drink. And Moses said unto them, Why chide ye [all of you] with me? Wherefore do ye tempt

Identifying the God of Abraham

the LORD?" Exodus 17:1, 2

Who is the Individual that led the children of Israel in a cloud, divided the sea, fed them, took them a place called Rephidim, and gave them water from a rock to drink?

The record states,

"₁ And all the congregation of the children of Israel journeyed from the wilderness of Sin, after their journeys, according to the commandment of the LORD, and pitched in Rephidim: and there was no water for the people to drink.

"₂ Wherefore the people did chide with Moses, and said, Give us water that we may drink. And Moses said unto them, Why chide ye with me? wherefore do ye [all of you] tempt the LORD?

"₃ And the people thirsted there for water; and the people murmured against Moses, and said, Wherefore is this that thou [you] hast brought us up out of Egypt, to kill us and our children and our cattle with thirst?

"₄ And Moses cried unto the LORD, saying, What shall I do unto this people? they be almost ready to stone me.
"₅ And the LORD said unto Moses, Go on before the people, and take with thee of the elders of Israel; and thy [your] rod, wherewith thou [you]

Identifying the God of Abraham

smotest the river, take in thine hand, and go.

"6 Behold, I will stand before thee [you] there upon the rock in Horeb; and thou [you] shalt smite the rock, and there shall come water out of it, that the people may drink.

"And Moses did so in the sight of the elders of Israel. 7 And he called the name of the place Massah, and Meribah, because of the chiding of the children of Israel, and because they tempted the LORD, saying, Is the LORD among us, or not?" (Exodus 17:1-7).

So! As per the above verses, who is the Individual that led the children of Israel in a cloud, divided the sea, fed them, and

Identifying the God of Abraham

gave them water to drink from a rock?

According to Apostle Paul's testimony, He is "the God of Israel," who is further identified by the character name of "Christ" (Χριστος) in 1 Corinthians 10:4

Here are the cross-references,

"1 MOREOVER, brethren, I would not that ye should be ignorant, how that all our fathers [the children of Israel] were under the cloud, and all passed though the sea;

"2 And were all baptized unto Moses in the cloud and in the sea;

"3 And did all eat the same spiritual meat;

*   "**4 *And did all drink the same spiritual drink: for they drank of that spiritual Rock that followed them: and that Rock was Christ [Χριστος]*"** (1 Corinthians 10:1-4).

And here are the above verses in the Greek text, which confirm the facts in v.4 that it was "Christ" (Χριστος) who gave them water to drink from a rock.

"1 ΔΕΝ θελω δε να αγνοητε, αδελφοι, οτι οι πατερες ημων ησαν παντες υπο την νεφελην, και παντες δια της θαλασσης διηλθον

"2 και παντες εις τον Μωυσην εβαπτισθησαν εν τη νεφελη και εν τη θαλασση

Identifying the God of Abraham

"₃ και παντες την αυτην πνευματικην βρωσιν εφαγον

* "₄ και παντες το αυτο πνευματικον ποτον επιον διοτι επινον απο πνευματικης πετρας ακολουθουσης η δε πετρα ητο ο Χριστος [Christ]." Προς Κορινθιους Α' 10:1-4 Βιβλικη Εταιρεια   1 Corinthians 10:1-4

As you can readily see in the (OKJV) of the Bible and in the Greek text above, in 1 Corinthians 10:4, Apostle Paul not only states that the Individual who gave the children of Israel water to drink from a rock (Exodus 17:1-6) was none other than *"Christ"* ("Χριστος"), but also, he further identifies Christ by His character name of "Rock," by saying, and that Rock that followed them: "was Christ [Χριστος]." 1 Corinthians 10:4

Therefore, we can conclude again, as per Moses' presentation and Apostle Paul's presentation, Christ ("Χριστος"), is the LORD God of Abraham and of the children of Israel. And since the LORD God of Abraham and of Israel is identified by Apostle Paul by the name of "Christ" (Χριστος), in 1 Corinthians 10:4, henceforth we can refer to Jesus Christ as the LORD God of Abraham and of Israel.

Meeting with the God of Abraham

After leaving Rephidim, Christ the LORD God of Abraham and of Israel, who was leading the children of Israel in the form of a cloud, led Jacob's descendents to the foot of Mount Sinai. There in the shadow of Mount Sinai, Israel set up camp in the usual disorganized manner. In order to correct the problem of discord and confusion, the children of Israel had to be organized for their journey to the Promised Land, and for their residence in the Promised Land. Therefore the mini structure of the camp of Israel, at the foot of Mount Sinai, was a structure of a larger picture, which was to take place in the Promised Land.

There, at the foot of Mount Sinai, while the children of Israel were erecting their camp, Moses was summoned by Christ the God of Abraham and of Israel to go up Mount Sinai and meet with Christ the LORD God of Abraham and of Israel. And, when Christ the LORD finished communicating with Moses, Moses came down from the mountain and asked the children of Israel if they wanted to meet with Christ the LORD God of their fathers, and enter into an agreement (Covenant) with Him? If the children of Israel did not want to enter into an agreement with Christ the God of their forefathers, Christ would not become their God, and the journey to the Promised Land would end there.

In response to Moses' question,

Meeting with the God of Abraham

> "⁸ all the people answered together, and said, All that the LORD hath spoken we will do."

And when Moses heard their response, he

> "returned the words of the people unto the LORD" (Exodus 19:8).

When Christ their God heard that the children of Israel wanted to enter into an agreement with Him, He told Moses to prepare the people to meet with Him in three days. They were to wash and assemble at the bottom border of Mount Sinai. They were to stand there at the foot of the mountain and not go up the mountain. And then, Christ the LORD God of Abraham and of Israel would come down upon Mount Sinai to meet with them.

> "⁹ And the LORD said unto Moses, Lo, I come unto thee [you] in a thick cloud, that the people may hear when I speak with thee [you], and believe thee [you] for ever " (Exodus 19:9).

After they agreed to meet with the LORD their God at the foot of Mount Sinai, three days later, the Covenant was given in an audible majestic presentation to the children of Israel, who were gathered at the foot of Mount Sinai; and that agreement was witnessed by the saints (holy angels) of God who hovered above and around Mount Sinai. In fact,

Meeting with the God of Abraham

> "8 The earth shook, the heavens also dropped at the presence of God: even Sinai itself was moved at the presence of God, the God of Israel" (Psalms 68:8).

As the majestic appearance took place upon Mount Sinai by Christ the LORD, He began to speak to the children of Israel by saying to them,

> "2 I am the LORD thy [your] God, which have brought thee [you] out of the land of Egypt, out of the house of bondage" (Exodus 20:2).

And, as Christ's words rolled down Mount Sinai, the earth under their feet trembled. And as the earth under their feet trembled and Mount Sinai moved out of its place, fear set in the children of Israel. But, nonetheless, Christ the LORD God of Israel continued speaking by saying,

I

> "3 Thou [you] shalt have no other gods before Me.

II

> "4 Thou [you] shalt not make unto thee [yourself] any graven image, or any likeness of any thing that is in heaven above, or that is in the earth beneath, or that is in the water under the earth: 5 Thou shalt not bow down thyself to them, nor serve them: for I the LORD thy God am a jealous God, visiting the

Meeting with the God of Abraham

iniquity of the fathers upon the children unto the third and fourth generation of them that hate Me; 6 And shewing mercy unto thousands of them that love Me, and keep My commandments.

III

"7 Thou [you] shalt not take the name of the LORD thy [Your] God in vain; for the LORD will not hold him guiltless that taketh His name in vain.

IV

"8 Remember the sabbath day, to keep it holy. 9 Six days shalt thou labour, and do all thy [your] work: 10 But the seventh day is the sabbath of the LORD thy God: in it thou shalt not do any work, thou, nor thy son, nor thy daughter, thy manservant, nor thy maidservant, nor thy cattle, nor thy stranger that is within thy gates: 11 For in six days the LORD made heaven and earth, the sea, and all that in them is, and rested the seventh day: wherefore the LORD blessed the sabbath day [Saturday], and hallowed it.

V

"12 Honour thy [your] father and thy mother: that thy days may be long upon the land which the LORD thy [Your] God giveth thee [you].

Meeting with the God of Abraham

VI
"₁₃ Thou [you] shalt not kill.

VII
"₁₄ Thou [you] shalt not commit adultery.

VIII
"₁₅ Thou [you] shalt not steal.

IX
"₁₆ Thou [you] shalt not bear false witness against thy neighbour.

X
"₁₇ Thou [you] shalt not covet thy [your] neighbour's house, thou shalt not covet thy neighbour's wife, nor his manservant, nor his maidservant, nor his ox, nor his ass, nor any thing that is thy neighbour's" (Exodus 20:3-17).

While the children of Israel and those who had joined the camp of Israel listened to each precept of the Decalogue, they were stunned and horrified of the awesome piercing words they were hearing. As the words of the Decalogue rolled down from the mountain and into the gathering of the people, the earth beneath their feet trembled and so did their hearts because each successive precept revealed more and more of the individual's sinful past acts.

Horrified at the revelation of their sinful acts, the people thought that it was retribution time! In their

Meeting with the God of Abraham

anxiety, they began to move away from the base of the mountain and shouted at Moses,

> "19 Speak thou [you] with us, and we will hear: but let not God speak with us, lest we die."

Seeing that the people were panic stricken, Moses stood before them, calmed them down, and said to them, "20 Fear not: for God is come to prove you, and that His fear may be before your faces, that ye [all of you] sin not" (Exodus 20:19, 20).

The above presentation was observed for miles around Mount Sinai; and those who observed it, outside of the camp of Israel, wondered what was taking place? But to the children of Israel who were below the mountain, they found it shocking! This was not what the children of Israel expected! Its impact left overwhelming impressions upon their hearts with mixed fearful lamentations.

The above Ten Commandments were not their foremost concern, while the children of Israel were in Egypt. The heathenish influence of the Egyptians took a toll in their holy lives, especially when Jacob (Israel) died. From his death and onward, the children of Israel gradually took to heart many of the heathenistic practices of the Egyptians. But during the last sixty years of their stay in Egypt, when the children of Israel were put into bondage by the new Pharaoh, many of the children of Israel forgot the God of their fathers.

Therefore, there was a greater divide amongst the people's faith in the God of their fathers, when they were forced into bondage by the Egyptians. Many drew

Meeting with the God of Abraham

closer to God of their fathers, while others slipped into a greater sinful degeneration. Therefore, they were in need to reflect upon these Ten Commandments and understand the penalty the Ten Commandments imposed upon the offender. And they were to also understand the need to stop breaking the Ten Commandments, in order to be a holy people unto Christ their God who took them out of Egypt. Christ the LORD said to the children of Israel, "Be ye [all of you] holy" (Leviticus 20:7).

The children of Israel were to put on the beautiful, beautiful character of Christ. They were to remain holy throughout their lives as a holy nation unto Christ the LORD, and as a beacon of light to a perishing world.

A number of days after their meeting with Christ the LORD of hosts, at the foot of Mount Sinai, Moses gathered the children of Israel in order to ratify the Covenant between them and Christ the LORD. Moses explained to the children of Israel that the Covenant contained the Ten Commandments and the ceremonial law. Therefore, before the children of Israel entered into a Covenant with Christ the LORD, Moses had an altar built with twelve pillars, one for each tribe of Israel, and offered burnt offerings to Christ the LORD; and when Moses asked the children of Israel if they wanted to enter into a Covenant with Christ the LORD God of their fathers, they said,

"3 All the words which the LORD hath said will we do" (Exodus 24:3).

Then Moses took some of the blood of the

Meeting with the God of Abraham

animals, which were sacrificed upon the altar, and sprinkled it upon the children of Israel. This act sealed the agreement with Christ their LORD. Moses said, "Behold the blood of the covenant."

Here are the references:

> "4 And Moses wrote all the words of the LORD, and rose up early in the morning, and builded an altar under the hill, and twelve pillars, according to the twelve tribes of Israel. 5 And he sent young men of the children of Israel, which offered burnt offerings, and sacrificed peace offerings of oxen unto the LORD.
>
> "6 And Moses took half of the blood, and put it in basons; and half of the blood he sprinkled on the altar.
>
> "7 And he took the book of the covenant, and read in the audience of the people: and they said,
>
>> "All that the LORD hath said will we do, and be obedient.
>
> "8 And Moses took the blood, and sprinkled it on the people, and said,
>
>> "Behold the blood of the covenant, which the LORD hath made with you concerning all these words," which Moses wrote in a book. (See Exodus 24:4-8)

Meeting with the God of Abraham

The Covenant, which the children of Israel entered in, with Christ the LORD God of their fathers, was ratified at the foot of Mount Sinai. It consisted of the Ten Commandments and the blood of the sacrificial animals (ceremonial law). This very same covenant, it should be known, was the same Covenant, which Christ the LORD of hosts presented to Adam and Eve, after their fall, in the Garden of Eden.

Furthermore, it should be remembered, the carnal ceremonial law was added because of sin; whereby, the Ten Commandments are spiritual and the standard by which the Government, of the Lawgiver (Christ), is based upon. The Creator's whole universe runs upon the holy Covenant of Love; it is based upon two standards.

1). Love the LORD God of His universe with all your heart in righteousness.

2). Love, in righteousness, your neighbor as yourself; and that means, not only the person next to you, but also, the person in the next galaxy and beyond. (See Matthew 22:40.)

When these two principles are upheld by us, we reside and uphold God's Government in righteousness and in love. If we abide by these two principles, in righteousness, we mean no malice to the human family, to the intelligent beings who reside throughout God's universe, outside of the universe, and to Christ the God of Israel, who created the universe. When these two principles are upheld, we will live in harmony with Christ and with His universe.

Meeting with the God of Abraham

It should also be noted; when we unfold these two principles of love (the two great Commandments), we end up with the Ten Commandments, as they were originally given to the human race, to abide by throughout eternity. (See Exodus 20:1-17.)

Scripture tells us "love is the fulfilling of the law" (Romans 13:10).

Furthermore, the ceremonial law consisted of washing, thank offerings, burnt offerings, sacrificial offerings, meat offerings, holy days, feast days, sabbatical days, sabbatical years, Day of Atonement, wave offering, etc., etc.; but, more importantly, there was the sacrificial animal offering on the altar of sacrifice for the remission of sins, which took place in the morning and in the evening. There, the penitent sinner would place his or her hand upon the animal's head, confess his or her sins, slay the animal by cutting its throat, and then, burn it on the altar of sacrifice.

After the Ten Commandments were presented audibly to the children of Israel, the children of Israel accepted the Covenant, which consisted of the carnal ceremonial law and the Ten holy Commandments, during their stay at the foot of Mount Sinai, which was in the early part of their first year of stay there. They said to Moses,

> "3 All the words which the LORD hath said will we do" (Exodus 24:3).

Once the children of Israel agreed to abide by the Covenant (Exodus 24:3), Christ the LORD God of Abraham became their God and they became His people. And when the children of Israel implemented

Meeting with the God of Abraham

the Covenant of Love in their lives, and asked for forgiveness for their sins, and were forgiven, they became a holy people unto Christ the LORD God of Israel. And as a holy people, Christ the God of Israel was able to dwell with His people in their camp.

Now that the camp of Israel chose to be sinless, Christ the LORD of hosts asked the children of Israel to build Him a Sanctuary so that He could "dwell among them." Christ said to Moses;

> "$_8$ And let them make Me a sanctuary; that I may dwell among them." Exodus 25:8

And Christ the LORD God of Israel added that He was going to meet with Moses and speak to Moses at the door of the tabernacle (tent).

Here is the account:

> "$_{42}$ This shall be a continual burnt offering throughout your generations at the door of the tabernacle of the congregation before the LORD:

> "where I will meet you [Moses], to speak there unto thee [you].

> "$_{43}$ And there I will meet with the children of Israel, and the tabernacle shall be sanctified by My glory. $_{44}$ And I will sanctify the tabernacle of the congregation, and the altar: I will sanctify also both Aaron and his sons, to minister to Me in the priest's office.

Meeting with the God of Abraham

"₄₅ And I will dwell among the children of Israel, and will be their God.

"₄₆ And they shall know that I am the LORD their God, that brought them forth out of the land of Egypt, that I may dwell among them: I am the LORD their God" (Exodus 29:42-46).

The children of Israel heard the LORD'S words and responded overwhelmingly. They did build for Christ the LORD their God a Sanctuary with all of its furniture and pitched it in the midst of the camp, in the first month (April) of the second year of stay, at the foot of Mount Sinai.

After they assembled the Sanctuary, so that the entrance faced to the east, they placed the furniture in the appropriate rooms of the tabernacle and in the courtyard. And when everything was in its proper place, the Sanctuary was dedicated to Christ the LORD God of their fathers who brought them out of the land of Egypt.

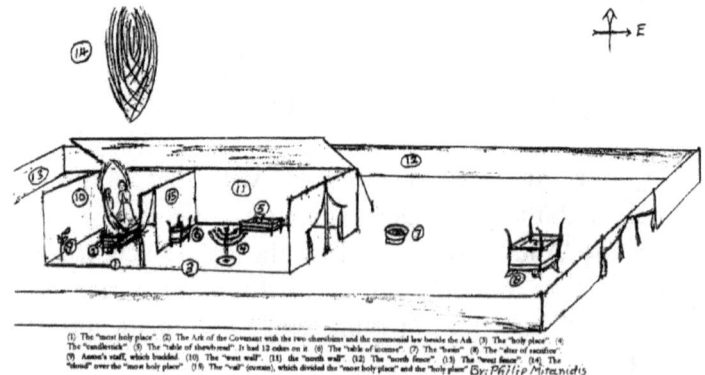

Meeting with the God of Abraham

Once the dedication took place, Christ the LORD God of Abraham and of Israel accepted the Sanctuary as His dwelling place, by filling the Sanctuary with His glory, and visibly remained above the "most holy place" of the tabernacle in a form of a cloud.

Now that the Sanctuary was occupied by the LORD God of Abraham and of Israel, there was a need to designate individuals for the maintenance of the Sanctuary.

Moses was advised by Christ the LORD God of Israel to set the tribe of Levi apart to look after the needs of the Sanctuary. There were groups designated to erect and dismantle the Sanctuary, a group to carry the furniture, a group to carry the fence, a group to carry the roof, a group to carry the Ark of the Covenant, and so on. And there was a group who was designated as priests for the Sanctuary. They were set apart to officiate in the Sanctuary's services before Christ the LORD God of Abraham who dwelt "in between the two cherubims," above the "mercy seat," in the "most holy place" of His Sanctuary.

Furthermore, Moses was to count all of the male children of Israel, who were above twenty years old, get a total of each tribe, and retain the totals in a book. And, when Moses and Aaron finished counting the number of people in each tribe, they were to also appoint "princes" (leaders) over every tribe. These leaders were the designated representatives of each tribe.

The record states that the counting took place on the first day of the second month in the second year of their stay in the wilderness of Sinai.

Meeting with the God of Abraham

Here is the account:

"₁₈ And they assembled all the congregation together on the first day of the second month, and they declared their pedigrees after their families, by the house of their fathers, according to the number of the names, from twenty years old and upward, by their polls. ₁₉ As the LORD commanded Moses, so he numbered them in the wilderness of Sinai" (Numbers 1:18, 19).

Here are the results:

"₂₁ Those that were numbered of them, even of the tribe of Reuben, were forty and six thousand and five hundred."

"₂₃ Those that were numbered of them, even of the tribe of Simeon, were fifty and nine thousand and three hundred."

"₂₅ Those that were numbered of them, even of the tribe of Gad, were forty and five thousand six hundred and fifty."

"₂₇ Those that were numbered of them, even of the tribe of Judah, were threescore and fourteen thousand and six hundred."

"₂₉ Those that were numbered of them, even of the tribe of Issachar, were fifty and four thousand and four hundred."

"₃₁ Those that were numbered of them, even of the tribe of Zebulun, were fifty and seven thousand and four hundred."

Meeting with the God of Abraham

"₃₃ Those that were numbered of them, even of the tribe of Ephraim, were forty thousand and five hundred."

"₃₅ Those that were numbered of them, even of the tribe of Manasseh, were thirty and two thousand and two hundred."

"₃₇ Those that were numbered of them, even of the tribe of Benjamin, were thirty and five thousand and four hundred."

"₃₉ Those that were numbered of them, even of the tribe of Dan, were threescore and two thousand and seven hundred."

"₄₁ Those that were numbered of them, even of the tribe of Asher, were forty and one thousand and five hundred."

"₄₃ Those that were numbered of them, even of the tribe of Naphtali, were fifty and three thousand and four hundred."

"₄₅ So were all those that were numbered of the children of Israel, by the house of their fathers, from twenty years old and upward, all that were able to go forth to war in Israel" (Numbers 1:21, 23, 25, 27, 29, 31, 33, 35, 37, 39, 41, 43, 45).

From the above tribes, the number of men from each tribe, over twenty years old, were as follows: 46,500 + 59,300 + 45,650 + 74,600 + 54,400 + 57,400 + 40,500 + 32,200 + 35,400 + 62,700 + 41,500 + 53,400. And when the above numbers are totaled, the number of soldiers who were able to go to war, and were over twenty years old, summed up to 609,550 souls.

After the counting of the soldiers was accomplished, and their leaders put in place, Moses told

Meeting with the God of Abraham

the various tribes of Israel to take their position and camp around the Sanctuary as they were ordered. There were three tribes positioned to the east of the Sanctuary. Three tribes camped to the south of the Sanctuary; three tribes camped to the west of the Sanctuary; three tribes camped to the north of the Sanctuary; and the tribe of Levi was camped in the center of the camp, around the Sanctuary.

This configuration was to be kept until they possessed and divided the Promised Land; and even then, the Sanctuary was to be placed in the middle of the children of Israel. And that place was called "Shiloh" (25 mi. north of the city of Jerusalem).

On the other hand, those individuals who were not Israelites and joined the children of Israel in their journey to the Promised Land, they were allowed to camp in the outer periphery of the camp of Israel. Their encampment, in that position, was to be maintained until such time they became fellow believers in the LORD God of Israel; and in time, they could join and dwell within the camp of Israel.

Here is a proximate presentation of the camp of Israel with the strangers who camped in the outer periphery of the tents of Israel.

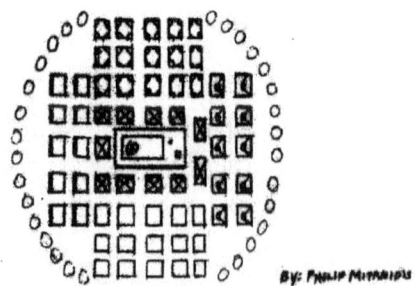

Meeting with the God of Abraham

There, in the wilderness of Mount Sinai, the children of Israel were gradually brought forward from disorganized groups, when they left Egypt, into an organized camp. There, the children of Israel met with Christ the God of their fathers, who brought them out of the land of Ur. There, the children of Israel met with Christ their God at the foot of Mount Sinai and made a Covenant with Him. There, at the foot of Sinai, the children of Israel accepted Christ the LORD God of their fathers, as their LORD and God. There, the children of Israel were disciplined and organized as a holy nation unto Christ the LORD God of Israel. There, the children of Israel were given the lively oracles (the 10 Commandments) of God in trust, to give unto us, and the mission to elevate Christ the LORD God of Israel before the unbelievers of the world, in order to bring hope and salvation to the lost souls of planet earth. They were to be ambassadors of Christ the LORD of hosts to the nations of the world. They were to share the Gospel message with the rest of the world that was given to Adam, to Abraham, and to them. They were to snatch lost souls from their adversary the devil and set them free into eternal life, by the grace of Christ the LORD God of Israel. There, in the wilderness of Sinai, Christ the LORD God of Abraham, Isaac, Jacob, and of the children of Israel confronted the children of Israel with the holy law of His universal Government. There, in the wilderness of Sinai, the children of Israel entered into an agreement (Covenant) with Christ their God, which meant that they would live a holy life by living within the precepts of the Covenant, which consisted of the holy spiritual Ten Commandments and the carnal ceremonial law. There,

Meeting with the God of Abraham

in the wilderness of Sinai, the blood of the Covenant was ratified, and the children of Israel accepted Christ the LORD God of their fathers, who brought them out of the land of Egypt, as their "LORD" and "God." There, in the wilderness of Sinai, the children of Israel built a Sanctuary for Christ their LORD God who brought them out of the land of bondage. There, in the wilderness of Sinai, Christ the mighty LORD God of Israel dwelt in the middle of the camp of Israel in the "most holy place" of His Sanctuary; which was surrounded by the tents of the Levite priests and by the remaining tents of the tribes of Israel. There, in the wilderness of Sinai, the children of Israel were counted, "15 made...captains over thousands, and captains over hundreds, and captains over fifties, and captains over tens, and officers among your tribes" (Deuteronomy 1:15). There, in the wilderness of Sinai, the children of Israel and those who joined the camp of Israel were organized and made ready to go and possess the Promised Land.

Now that the children of Israel were organized, and their lives dedicated to Christ their LORD God who brought them out of bondage, they were ready to follow Christ their LORD God who dwelt in His Sanctuary, in the middle of the camp of Israel.

After the numbering of the male children of Israel, who were over twenty years old, was accomplished, a number of days later, the cloud that was hovering above the "most holy place" of the tabernacle (tent) began to move away from the Sanctuary and outward from the camp of Israel.

When Moses, Aaron, and the rest of the children of Israel observed the moving cloud, they began to

Meeting with the God of Abraham

dismantle their tents and made ready to move onward wherever the cloud was to lead them.

First the Levi priests went into the "most holy place" of the tabernacle, picked up the Ark of the Covenant, and began to follow the cloud where it had stopped in a distance. Then the Levites, who were given the task of assembling and disassembling the Sanctuary followed; after the furniture was removed from the "most holy place," from the "holy place," and from the courtyard by the appointed groups of Levites.

When the Levites were ready to go forward with the dismantled Sanctuary and follow the Ark of the Covenant from a distance, about 300 meters, then the three tribes of the north followed the tribe of Levi from a short distance. After them, the three tribes from the east followed the three tribes of the north. And likewise, the three tribes of the south followed the three tribes from the east sector of the camp. And the three tribes from the west followed the three tribes from the south. And lastly, the strangers who were camped in the periphery of Israel's camp followed at the end.

We are told,

> "36 when the cloud was taken up from over the tabernacle, the children of Israel went onward in all their journeys: 37 But if the cloud were not taken up, then they journeyed not till the day that it was taken up. 38 For the cloud of the LORD was upon the tabernacle by day, and fire was on it by night, in the sight of all the house of Israel, throughout all their journeys" (Exodus 40:36-38).

At Kadesh-barnea

A person could see the camp of Israel moving forward in an organized and orderly manner following their leader, Christ the LORD God of Israel, who was in the cloud, above the Ark of the Covenant. He was leading them northeast from Mount Sinai to the Wilderness of Paran, to a place called Kadesh-barnea.

AT KADESH-BARNEA

When the children of Israel arrived at Kadesh-barnea, Christ the God of Israel, who was leading the children of Israel in a cloud, stopped there. And when the children of Israel saw in a distance that the Levi priests who were carrying the Ark of the Covenant stopped, it indicated to the children of Israel to stop and prepare to camp. And the reason Christ the God of Israel wanted the children of Israel to camp there was to have the camp of Israel prepare for their journey into the Promised Land, which was a stone throw away from the Hebrew's camp (the children of Israel).

But, before they ventured in the Promised Land, the children of Israel sent twelve spies in it, in order to assess the people who lived there and the land.

And when the twelve spies returned to Kadesh-barnea, ten of the spies gave a very negative report. In

At Kadesh-barnea

fact, it was so negative that it discouraged the children of Israel from going forward into the land.

After the negative report, Christ the God of Israel still wanted the children of Israel to go and possess the land. They were told to go northward and forward and possess the land of Canaan. Instead, they refused to go forward because they were afraid from the giants who posed the land.

Moses writes:

> "32 And they [the spies] brought up an evil report of the land which they had searched unto the children of Israel, saying, The land, through which we have gone to search it, is a land that eateth up the inhabitants thereof; and all the people that we saw in it are men of a great stature.
>
>> "33 And there we saw the giants, the sons of Anak, which come of the giants: and we were in our own sight as grasshoppers, and so we were in their sight." Numbers 13:32, 33

> "1 And all the congregation lifted up their voice, and cried; and the people wept that night. 2 And all the children of Israel murmured against Moses and against Aaron: and the whole congregation said unto them, Would God that we had died in the land of Egypt! or would God we had died in this wilderness! 3 And wherefore

At Kadesh-barnea

hath the LORD brought us unto this land, to fall by the sword, that our wives and our children should be a prey? were it not better for us to return into Egypt?" (Numbers 14:1-3).

Therefore, the children of Israel purposed to go back to Egypt. But, after a short hoopla, reality set in, and realized without the leadership and protection of Christ the God of Israel, they would not survive the trip. And, if they were to survive the trip, would Pharaoh welcome them back into his kingdom?

Finally after a horrible ordeal and confrontation with Christ their God, the children of Israel chose to wander in the wilderness for thirty-eight years before their children finally chose to go and inherit the land.

Here are the references,

"1 And all the congregation lifted up their voice, and cried; and the people wept that night. 2 And all the children of Israel murmured against Moses and against Aaron: and the whole congregation said unto them, Would God that we had died in the land of Egypt! or would God we had died in this wilderness! 3 And wherefore hath the LORD brought us unto this land, to fall by the sword, that our wives and our children should be a prey? were it not better for us to return into Egypt?

"4 And they said one to another, Let us make a captain, and let us return into Egypt.

At Kadesh-barnea

"5 Then Moses and Aaron fell on their faces before all the assembly of the congregation of the children of Israel. 6 And Joshua the son of Nun, and Caleb the son of Jephunneh, which were of them that searched the land, rent their clothes: 7 And they spake unto all the company of the children of Israel, saying, The land, which we passed through to search it, is an exceeding good land. 8 If the LORD delight in us, then He will bring us into this land, and give it us; a land which floweth with milk and honey. 9 Only rebel not ye [all of you] against the LORD, neither fear ye the people of the land; for they are bread for us: their defense is departed from them, and the LORD is with us: fear them not.

"10 But all the congregation bade stone them with stones. And the glory of the LORD appeared in the tabernacle of the congregation before all the children of Israel. 11 And the LORD said unto Moses, How long will this people provoke me? and how long will it be ere they believe Me, for all the signs which I have shewed among them?" Numbers 14:1-11

How long would the children of Israel provoke Christ the LORD God of Israel? Well, obviously He knows, but to make the point of their impatient rebellious ways, the LORD God of Israel said to Moses, these people already have tempted Me ten times!
    Can you imagine their aggressive rebellious attitude towards Christ their LORD?
    Since they tempted Christ their God ten times in

At Kadesh-barnea

such a short period of time, what were they going to be like in the thirty-eight years of wandering in the dessert?

During their thirty-ninth year, a continuation of temptations.

In His mercy Christ the God of Israel did not abandon the children of Israel at Kadesh-barnea. He took the children of Israel throughout the wilderness for thirty-eight years. And during those thirty-eight years, He provided food and water for them, protected their clothing, and their shoes from wearing out. He also protected them from disease, protected their feet from swelling, protected them from poisonous creepy crawlies, protected them from the heat and cold, and protected them from their enemies. But, the children of Israel continued to be rebellious and provocative towards Moses, Aaron, and Christ the LORD who was looking after their well being.

The prophet of the LORD writes, regarding their overall unfaithful attitude towards Christ the LORD, starting from a place called Migdol.

"18 And they tempted God in their heart by asking meat for their lust. 19 Yea, they spake against God; they said, Can God furnish a table in the wilderness?

"20 Behold, he smote the rock, that the waters gushed out, and the streams overflowed; can He give bread also? can He provide flesh for His people?

At Kadesh-barnea

"₂₁ Therefore the LORD heard this, and was wroth: so a fire was kindled against Jacob, and anger also came up against Israel; ₂₂ Because they believed not in God, and trusted not in His salvation:

"₂₃ Though He had commanded the clouds from above, and opened the doors of heaven, "₂₄ And had rained down manna upon them to eat, and had given them of the corn of heaven. ₂₅ Man did eat angels' food: He sent them meat to the full. ₂₆ He caused an east wind to blow in the heaven: and by His power He brought in the south wind. ₂₇ He rained flesh also upon them as dust, and feathered fowls like as the sand of the sea: ₂₈ And He let it fall in the midst of their camp, round about their habitations. ₂₉ So they did eat, and were well filled: for He gave them their own desire; ₃₀ They were not estranged from their lust. But while their meat was yet in their mouths, ₃₁ The wrath of God came upon them, and slew the fattest of them, and smote down the chosen men of Israel.

"₃₂ For all this they sinned still, and believed not for His wondrous works.

"₃₃ Therefore their days did He consume in vanity, and their years in trouble. ₃₄ When He slew them, then they sought Him: and they returned and enquired early after God. ₃₅ And they remembered that God was their Rock, and

At Kadesh-barnea

the High God their Redeemer.

> "36 Nevertheless they did flatter Him with their mouth, and they lied unto Him with their tongues.
>
> "37 For their heart was not right with Him, neither were they stedfast in His covenant.
>
> "38 But He, being full of compassion, forgave their iniquity, and destroyed them not: yea, many a time turned He His anger away, and did not stir up all His wrath." Psalms 78:18-38

And on their thirty-ninth year, the attitude of the children of Israel did not change. They tempted Christ the LORD God of Israel even more.

The record states,

> "40 How oft did they provoke Him in the wilderness, and grieve Him in the desert! 41 Yea, they turned back and tempted God, and limited the Holy One [Christ] of Israel. 42 They remembered not His hand, nor the day when He delivered them from the enemy." Psalms 78:40-42

> "56 Yet they tempted and provoked the Most High God [Christ], and kept not His testimonies: 57 But turned back, and dealt unfaithfully like their fathers: they were turned aside like a

At Kadesh-barnea

deceitful bow." Psalms 78:56, 57

According to the above verses, the children of Israel tempted and provoked Christ the LORD God of Israel numerous times during their travels in wilderness. And in reference to that period of time, Apostle Paul makes mention in summary of the callous unbelieving hearts of the children of Israel towards Christ the LORD God of Israel by saying,

"5 But with many of them God [Christ, see 1 Corinthians 10:4, 9] was not well pleased: for they were overthrown in the wilderness.

"6 Now these things were our examples, to the intent we should not lust after evil things, as they also lusted.

"7 Neither be ye [all of you] idolaters, as were some of them; as it is written, The people sat down to eat and drink, and rose up to play.

"8 Neither let us commit fornication, as some of them committed, and fell in one day three and twenty thousand" (1 Corinthians 10:5-8).

Like the Psalmist (Psalms 78), Apostle Paul, in 1 Corinthians 10:1-10, also summarizes the events of the Torah and the temptation that are revealed to us by the pen of Moses; and in his summary, Apostle Paul reveals, with many of the children of Israel, "God [Christ] was not well pleased." And, he also adds that twenty-three thousand of the children of Israel fell in

At Kadesh-barnea

one day because they committed fornication (v.8).

But, the children of Israel, for one reason or another, did not stop tempting Christ the LORD. On their thirty-ninth year, when they reached the borders of Edom, they ran out of rations and water.

What happened to the children of Israel was the refusal by the King of Edom, who was a descendant of Esau, to accommodate the children of Israel to go through Edom's land and take the highway northward to Moabite country. And that refusal by the king of Edom forced Moses to take the children of Israel and travel west of the border of Edom and go northward to the southern tip of the Dead Sea, in order to cross over the Brook Zered and into Moabite country, which is east of the Dead Sea.

What ensued during their stop at the border of Edom, before they crossed the Brook Zered, the children of Israel ran out of food and water. And in their impatient frenzy, they rebelled against Christ to such a wicked and ugly state that Christ the "LORD God of Israel" had to leave His Sanctuary in order to avoid the destruction of the camp of Israel because of their perpetual sins.

And when Christ left the camp of Israel, His protection left with Him. And when Satan saw that Christ was not protecting the children of Israel anymore, Satan and his evil angels coerced the snakes and scorpions to attack the children of Israel. And when they did, twenty-three thousand died in one day before the attack was stopped.

Here are the references from the Old Testament,

"[4] And they journeyed from mount Hor by the

At Kadesh-barnea

way of the Red sea, to compass the land of Edom: and the soul of the people was much discouraged because of the way.

"₅ And the people spake against God, and against Moses, Wherefore have ye brought us up out of Egypt to die in the wilderness? for there is no bread, neither is there any water; and our soul loatheth this light bread.

*
> "₆ *And the LORD sent fiery serpents among the people, and they bit the people; and much people of Israel died.*

"₇ Therefore the people came to Moses, and said, We have sinned, for we have spoken against the LORD, and against thee [you]; pray unto the LORD, that he take away the serpents from us. And Moses prayed for the people." Numbers 21:4-7

Finally the children of Israel acknowledged their sins and turned to Moses and said to him, "We have sinned, for we have spoken against the LORD, and against thee [you]; pray unto the LORD, that He take away the serpents from us. And Moses prayed for the people." And when Moses prayed on their behalf, Christ the God of Israel removed the scorpions and the poisonous snakes from the camp of Israel.

After the camp settled down, the people took the time and buried their dead.

Here are the cross-references of the above

136   Christ's Sovereignty......... *By: Philip Mitanidis*
At Kadesh-barnea

events taken from the New Testament, which reveal to whom the children of Israel "spake against," and who was the "God" they were tempting? Noticeably, according to the following verses, written by Apostle Paul, it was Christ the LORD God of Israel. He says,

* "9 *Neither let us temp Christ [Χριστος], as some of them also tempted, and were destroyed of serpents.*

 "10 Neither murmur ye, as some of them also murmured, and were destroyed of the destroyer [Satan]" (1 Corinthians 10:9, 10).

And here are the above verses in the Greek text, which testify to the fact that the children of Israel tempted Christ (Χριστον) the LORD God of Israel, and caused Satan to have a free hand to coerce the snakes and scorpions to bite the children of Israel near the border of Edom.

* "9 *Μηδε ας πειραζωμεν τον Χριστον [Christ], καθως και τινες αυτων επειρασαν, και απωλεσθησαν υπο των οφεων.*

 "10 Μηδε γογγυζετε, καθως και τινες αυτων εγογγυσαν, και απωλεσθησαν υπο του εξολοθρευτου." Προς Κορινθιους Α' Βιβλικη Εταιρεια 1 Corinthians 10:9, 10

As per the above verses (Numbers 21:4-6; 1 Corinthians 10:9), the Individual who was tempted by

Crossing the Jordan River

the children of Israel, while He was leading the children of Israel along the borders of Edom, according to Apostle Paul, was Christ ("Χριστος" 1 Corinthians 10:9), better known to the children of Israel by the name of the "LORD God of Israel."

According to all of the above cross-references, which I have provided for you, as you have read, there is only one LORD, and that LORD is Christ the LORD God of Abraham and of the children of Israel who led them in a cloud from Raamses and into the borders of the Promised Land.

Crossing the Jordan River into Gilgal

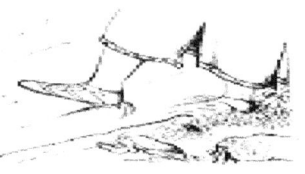

On their fortieth year, a handful of the children of those who were counted, and those who were not counted, crossed the Brook Zerid into Moabite country; and eventually reached Shittim, after Moses saw the Promised Land, from Mount Nebo, which is on the eastern side of the Jordan River—he died there.

After Moses' death, the task of leadership and authority was given to Joshua. He was to lead the children of Israel across the Jordan River, into the land of Canaan, and remain as their leader until his death.

Although Christ the LORD God of Israel chose

Crossing the Jordan River

Joshua to be their leader, his leadership of success and failure was conditional, as it was conditional with Moses.

Christ the LORD said unto Joshua, "2 Moses My servant is dead; now therefore arise, go over this Jordan, thou [you], and all this people, unto the land which I do give to them, even to the children of Israel. 3 Every place that the sole of your foot shall tread upon, that have I given unto you, as I said unto Moses. 4 From the wilderness and this Lebanon even unto the great river, the river Euphrates, all the land of the Hittites, and unto the great sea toward the going down of the sun, shall be your coast."

Then the LORD made a promise to Joshua by saying, "5 There shall not any man be able to stand before thee [you] all the days of thy life: as I was with Moses, so I will be with thee: I will not fail thee, nor forsake thee. 6 Be strong and of a good courage: for unto this people shalt thou [you] divide for an inheritance the land, which I sware unto their fathers to give them."

Then, God the Christ set forth the conditions for Joshua's success. If Joshua met the following conditions, the above promises would be fulfilled by Christ the LORD God of Israel. The LORD said to Joshua, "7 Only be thou [you] strong and very courageous, that thou mayest observe to do according to all the law, which Moses My servant commanded thee [you]: turn not from it to the right hand or to the left, that thou [you] mayest prosper whithersoever thou goest.

"8 This book of the law shall not depart out of

Crossing the Jordan River

> thy [your] mouth; but thou [you] shalt meditate therein day and night, that thou mayest observe to do according to all that is written therein: for then thou shalt make thy [your] way prosperous, and then thou [you] shalt have good success" (Joshua 1:2-8).

The standard that was set for Joshua was the same standard that was set for Moses and for all of the children of Israel. Joshua had to abide and uphold the Covenant and teach the children of Israel to do the same. If Joshua did that, he and the children of Israel would prosper continually in the land, which Christ the LORD their God was going to give them.

When Joshua presented the blessings, and the condition of those blessings to the children of Israel, the children of Israel responded by saying to Joshua,

> "16 All that thou [you] commandest us we will do, and whithersoever thou sendest us, we will go. 17 According as we hearkened unto Moses in all things, so will we hearken unto thee [you]: only the LORD thy [your] God be with thee [you], as He was with Moses" (Joshua 1:16, 17).

When Joshua heard the blessings from the children of Israel, and their willing support to his leadership, he said to the children of Israel that very soon they will cross over the River Jordan; and eventually, they would possess the rest of the Promised Land.

Crossing the Jordan River

I used the word "eventually" because the LORD did not want to drive all of the inhabitants away from their land at once. The reason why the LORD did not want to drive the inhabitants away at once was due to the fact that He did not want the land to turn wild and unbearable. Christ the LORD said,

> "29 I will not drive them out from before thee [you] in one year; lest the land become desolate, and the beast of the field multiply against thee [you]" (Exodus 23:29).

But before they crossed the River Jordan, Joshua commanded that two spies be sent into the city of Jericho and obtain as much information about the people who live in the city and in the surrounding area.

When the spies entered into Jericho, as inconspicuous as they tried to be that they were not foreigners, they were spotted and reported to the authorities. In the interim, the authorities reported the matter to the king, and the king of Jericho hastened his soldiers to intercept the two intruders, who were in the harlot's house, named Rahab. When the soldiers came to Rahab's house, she took the two spies and hid them on top of the flat roof under a pile of flax; and then, she came to the soldiers to answer their questions. In reply, she said to them, "The Hebrews were here, but when they heard that you were coming, they fled down the window and went towards the city gate."

When the soldiers heard what happened, they rushed towards the gate and told the gate kippers to shut the gates after they went out. While the soldiers

Crossing the Jordan River

searched outside of the city for the Hebrews, Rahab went to the two spies who were under the flax and told them to come out. When they came out from the pile of flax "9 she said unto the men, I know that the LORD hath given you the land, and that your terror is fallen upon us, and that all the inhabitants of the land faint because of you. 10 For we have heard how the LORD dried up the water of the Red sea for you, when ye came out of Egypt; and what ye did unto the two kings of the Amorites, that were on the other side Jordan [east-side of the River Jordan], Sihon and Og, whom ye utterly destroyed.

> "11 And as soon as we had heard these things, our hearts did melt, neither did there remain any more courage in any man, because of you: for the LORD your God, He is God in heaven above, and in earth beneath.

> "12 Now therefore, I pray you, swear unto me by the LORD, since I have shewed you kindness that ye will also shew kindness unto my father's house, and give me a true token: 13 And that ye [allof you] will save alive my father, and my mother, and my brethren, and my sisters, and all that they have, and deliver our lives from death. 14 And the men answered her, Our life for yours, if ye utter not this our business. And it shall be, when the LORD hath given us the land, that we will deal kindly and truly with thee.

> "15 Then she let them down by a cord through the window: for her house was upon the town wall, and she dwelt upon the wall. 16 And she said unto them, Get

Crossing the Jordan River

you to the mountain, lest the pursuers meet you; and hide yourselves there three day, until the pursuers be returned: and afterward may ye go your way. 17 And the men said unto her, We will be blameless of this thine [your] oath which thou [you] hast made us swear. 18 Behold, when we come into the land, thou shalt bind this line of scarlet thread in the window which thou didst let us down by: and thou shalt bring thy father, and thy mother, and thy brethren, and all thy father's household, home unto thee. 19 And it shall be, that whosoever shall go out of the doors of thy [your] house into the street, his blood shall be upon his head, and we will be guiltless: and whosoever shall be with thee in the house, his blood shall be on our head, if any hand be upon him. 20 And if thou utter this our business, then we will be quit of thine oath which thou hast made us to swear. 21 And she said, According unto your words, so be it. And she sent them away, and they departed: and she bound the scarlet line in the window. 22 And they went, and came unto the mountain, and abode there three days, until the pursuers were returned: and the pursuers sought them throughout all the way, but found them not" (Joshua 2:9-22).

One of the predominant observation by the two Hebrew spies was the fact that they heard how fearful the inhabitants of the land were because the Hebrews were coming their way. And when

> "23 the two men returned, and descended from the mountain, and passed over, and came to Joshua the son of Nun, and told him all things that befell them: 24 And they said unto Joshua, Truly the LORD

Crossing the Jordan River

hath delivered into our hands all the land; for even all the inhabitants of the country do faint because of us" (Joshua 2:23, 24).

The next day, "1 Joshua rose early in the morning; and they removed from Shittim, and came to Jordan, he and all the children of Israel, and lodged there before they passed over." And the leaders of the tribes of Israel said to the people. "3 When ye see the ark of the covenant of the LORD your God, and the priests the Levites bearing it, then ye shall remove from your place, and go after it [follow it]. 4 Yet there shall be a space between you and it, about two thousand cubits by measure [about 2/3 mi.]: come not near unto it, that ye may know the way by which ye must go: for ye have not passed this way heretofore. 5 And Joshua said unto the people, Sanctify yourselves: for to morrow the LORD will do wonders among you." And then, Joshua added, "9 Come hither, and hear the words of the LORD your God." When you see "11 the ark of the covenant of the LORD of all the earth passeth over before you into Jordan. 12 Now therefore take you twelve men out of the tribes of Israel, out of every tribe a man. 13 And it shall come to pass, as soon as the soles of the feet of the priests that bear the ark of the LORD, the LORD of all the earth, shall rest in the waters of Jordan, that the waters of Jordan shall be cut off from the waters that come down

Crossing the Jordan River

from above; and they shall stand upon an heap.

"₁₄ And it came to pass, when the people removed from their tents, to pass over Jordan, and the priests bearing the ark of the covenant before the people; ₁₅ And as they that bare the ark were come unto Jordan, and the feet of the priests that bare the ark were dipped in the brim of the water, (for Jordan overfloweth all his banks all the time of harvest,) ₁₆ That the waters which came down from above stood and rose up upon an heap very far from the city Adam, that is beside Zaretan: and those that came down toward the sea of the plain, even the salt sea, failed, and were cut off: and the people passed over right against Jericho. ₁₇ And the priest that bare the ark of the covenant of the LORD stood firm on dry ground in the midst of Jordan, and all the Israelites passed over on dry ground, until all the people were passed clean over Jordan" (Joshua 3:1, 3-5, 9, 11-17).

And when all of the children of Israel passed to the other side of the River Jordan safely, Joshua "₁₇ commanded the priests, saying, Come ye [all of you] up out of Jordan. ₁₈ And it came to pass, when the priests that bare the ark of the covenant of the LORD were come up out of the midst of Jordan, and the soles of the priests' feet were lifted up unto the dry land, that the waters of Jordan returned unto their place, and flowed over all his banks, as they did before. ₁₉ And the people came up out of Jordan on the tenth day of the first month, and encamped in Gilgal, in the east border of Jericho. ₂₀ And those twelve stones, which they took out of Jordan, did Joshua pitch in Gilgal" (Joshua 4:17-20).

When the children of Israel arrived at Gilgal, in

Crossing the Jordan River

the forty-first year of their journey, they camped there. And while they were at Gilgal, Christ the LORD wanted the children of Israel to be circumcised and to keep the Passover. The LORD said to Joshua, "2 Make thee sharp knives, and circumcise again the children of Israel the second time. 3 And Joshua made him sharp knives, and circumcised the children of Israel at the hill of the foreskins. 4 And this is the cause why Joshua did circumcise: All the people that came out of Egypt, that were males, even all the men of war, died in the wilderness by the way, after they came out of Egypt. 5 Now all the people that came out were circumcises: but all the people that were born in the wilderness by the way as they came forth out of Egypt, them they had not circumcises. 6 For the children of Israel walked forty years in the wilderness, till all the people that were men of war, which came out of Egypt, were consumed, because they obeyed not the voice of the LORD: unto whom the LORD sware that He would not shew them the land, which the LORD sware unto their fathers that He would give us, a land that floweth with milk and honey. 7 And their children, whom He raised up in their stead, them Joshua circumcised: for they were uncircumcised, because they had not circumcised them by the way. 8 And it came to pass, when they had done circumcising all the people, that they abode in their places in the camp, till they were whole [healed]. 9 And the LORD said unto Joshua, This day have I rolled away the reproach of Egypt from off you. Wherefore the name of the place is called Gilgal unto this day. 10 And the children of Israel encamped in Gilgal, and kept the passover on the fourteenth day of the month at even in the plains of Jericho. 11 And they did eat of the old

Crossing the Jordan River

corn of the land on the morrow after the passover, unleavened cakes, and parched corn in the selfsame day. 12 And the manna ceased on the morrow after they had eaten of the old corn of the land; neither had the children of Israel manna any more; but they did eat of the fruit of the land of Canaan that year" (Joshua 5:2-12).

After the children of Israel settled in Gilgal and were feeding from the land, the LORD told Joshua to go and overthrow Jericho as his first assignment in the west side of Jordan. Joshua was to remove from the land of Canaan all those individuals who did not want to join the LORD'S camp. And when the army of Israel did enter into Jericho, they also kept their promise to Rahab the harlot. As it was promised to her, she and her household were spared from death.

When the kings of the Amalekites and the Canaanites, Amorites, Hittites, Perizzites, Hivites, Jebusites, and so on, heard what happened to Jericho, they were terrified. They wondered; how could a city so strong fall by the hands of the Hebrews? And what about them, were they able to withstand their attack?

They watched the moves of the Hebrews, and were dismayed because now, another city fell by the name of "Ai." They wondered who was next on their list.

Soon after, the children of Israel returned to Gilgal and waited for Christ the LORD to direct them where to strike next. As they waited upon the LORD, they were visited by a caravan, which appeared that it had traveled a long distance. As they entered the camp of Israel, a person could see that the strangers had dusty old worn out sacks on their animals, shabby blankets,

Crossing the Jordan River

old wine bottles, and uneatable bread. In fact the bread was so old that it was hard, moldy, and indigestible. Their clothes were tattered, stinky, and old. Their shoes, likewise, were worn out and some had them patched with cloth. Their animals looked tired, dusty, and moved slowly in the camp, as they were led in the direction of Joshua.

After they were greeted by Joshua, they were asked where did they come from? They replied that they had come from a far country, and the reason why they came to them was to make peace with Israel. They said that they had heard the fame of their LORD God and what He did to the Egyptians and to the kings who were on the east side of the River Jordan. Therefore, they said that the elders of their country sent them to make peace with them and sware that no harm would come to them when they came.

As it turned out, as it was with the first attack on the city of "Ai," the children of Israel did not ask the LORD for guidance whether to make peace with these strangers or not. Instead, Joshua and the elders swore to the strangers that they and their countrymen would not be harmed. In "Ai," the children of Israel lost the war and a multitude of their men; this time, the children of Israel were fortunate that the Gibeonites did submit themselves to the children of Israel; and no lives were lost. But, it makes one wonder how could the children of Israel bypass Christ the LORD their God, who resided with them, and go contrary to His command, which said that they were not to make a league with strangers?

Should they not consult with the LORD their God first? The answer is obviously, yes they should!

Crossing the Jordan River

But since they did not, they had to live with their own decision.

Here is the incident, which led to Joshua's decision: "3 And when the inhabitants of Gibeon heard what Joshua had done unto Jericho and to Ai, 4 They did work wilily, and went and made as if they had been ambassadors, and took old sacks upon their asses, and wine bottles, old, and rent, and bound up; 5 And old shoes and clouted upon their feet, and old garments upon them; and all the bread of their provision was dry and mouldy. 6 And they went to Joshua unto the camp at Gilgal, and said unto him, and to the men of Israel, We be [are] come from a far country: now therefore make ye a league with us. 7 And the men of Israel said unto the Hivites, Peradventure ye dwell among us; and how shall we make a league with you? 8 And they said unto Joshua, We are thy [your] servants. And Joshua said unto them, Who are ye [all of you]? and from whence come ye? 9 And they said unto him, From a very far country thy servants are come because of the name of the LORD thy God: for we have heard the fame of Him, and all that He did in Egypt, 10 And all that He did to the two kings of the Amorites, that were beyond Jordan [east of Jordan], to Sihon king of Heshbon, and to Og king of Bashan, which was at Ashtaroth. 11 Wherefore our elders and all the inhabitants of our country spake to us, saying, Take victuals [food] with you for the journey, and go to meet them, and say unto them, We are your servants: therefore now make ye a league with us." "14 And the men took of their victuals, and asked not counsel at the mouth of the LORD. 15 And Joshua made peace with them, and made a league with them, to let them live:

Crossing the Jordan River

and the princes of the congregation sware unto them. 16 And it came to pass at the end of three days after they had made a league with them, that they heard that they were their neighbours, and that they dwelt among them. 17 And the children of Israel journeyed, and came unto their cities on the third day. Now their cities were Gibeon, and Chephirah, and Beeroth, and Kirjathjearim. 18 And the children of Israel smote them not, because the princes of the congregation had sworn unto them by the LORD God of Israel. And all the congregation murmured against the princes. 19 But all the princes said unto all the congregation, We have sworn unto them by the LORD God of Israel: now therefore we may not touch them. 20 This we will do to them; we will even let them live, lest wrath be upon us, because of the oath which we sware unto them" (Joshua 9:3-11, 14-20).

But even worse, when the kings of Canaan learned that Israel let the Gibeonites live because they made a league with them, they were in disbelief! The Canaanites could not understand why the inhabitants of one of the mightiest cities, called Gibeon, Joined God's people? The kings of Canaan were so mad that they became defiant towards Gibeon and Israel. To their disapproval and hate towards the Gibeonites, the Canaanites chose to join forces and eradicate the Gibeonites, or Hivites if you like.

Here is the account: When the king of Jerusalem "1 heard how Joshua had taken Ai, and had utterly destroyed it; as he had done to Jericho and her king, so he had done to Ai and her king; and how the inhabitants of Gibeon had made peace with Israel, and were among them; 2 That they feared greatly, because Gibeon was a great city, as one of the royal cities, and because it was

Crossing the Jordan River

greater than Ai, and all the men thereof were mighty. 3 Wherefore Adonizedec king of Jerusalem sent unto Hoham king of Hebron, and unto Piram king of Jarmuth, and unto Japhia king of Lachish, and unto Debir king of Eglon, saying, 4 Come up unto me, and help me, that we may smite Gibeon: for it hath made peace with Joshua and with the children of Israel. 5 Therefore the five kings of the Amorites, the king of Jerusalem, the king of Hebron, the king of Jarmuth, the king of Lachish, the king of Eglon, gathered themselves together, and went up, they and all their hosts, and encamped before Gibeon, and made war against it" (Joshua 10:1-5).

When the men of Gibeon saw that they were outnumbered, they sent word to Joshua asking him for help. They said, "6 Slack not thy hand from thy servants; come up to us quickly, and save us, and help us: for all the kings of the Amorites that dwell in the mountains are gathered together against us. 7 So Joshua ascended from Gilgal, he, and all the people of war with him, and all the mighty men of valour. 8 And the LORD said unto Joshua, Fear them not: for I have delivered them into thine [your] hand; there shall not a man of them stand before thee. 9 Joshua therefore came unto them suddenly, and went up from Gilgal all night. 10 And the LORD discomfited them before Israel, and slew them with a great slaughter at Gibeon, and chased them along the way that goeth up to Bethhoron, and smote them to Azekah, and unto Makkedah. 11 And it came to pass, as they fled from before Israel, and were in the going down to Bethhoron, that the LORD cast down great stones from heaven upon them unto Azekah, and they died: they were more which died with

Crossing the Jordan River

hailstones than they whom the children of Israel slew with the sword. 12 Then spake Joshua to the LORD in the day when the LORD delivered up the Amorites before the children of Israel, and he said in the sight of Israel, Sun, stand thou [you] still upon Gibeon; and thou, Moon, in the valley of Ajalon.

> "13 And the sun stood still, and the moon stayed, until the people had avenged themselves upon their enemies, Is not this written in the book of Jasher? So the sun stood still in the midst of heaven, and hasted not to go down about a whole day.

"14 And there was no day like that before it or after it, that the LORD hearkened unto the voice of a man: for the LORD fought for Israel. 15 And Joshua returned, and all Israel with him, unto the camp to Gilgal" (Joshua 10:6-15).

Shortly after the enemy dispersed, word came to Joshua that the five kings who fled from the army of Israel were found in a cave. Joshua said to the soldiers to seal the mouth of the cave, and keep the kings inside the cave. When Joshua arrived at the site, he commanded his soldiers to bring the five kings before him. When they did, he told them to place their feet upon their necks and kill them. After that, they were to hang them upon five trees, as a witness to the rest of the kings in the land who planed to oppose the Israelites.

Hearing the defeat of the five kings, the remaining kings of the land trembled at the advances the Hebrews were making in their land by the

Crossing the Jordan River

leadership of Joshua.

Slowly, over a year, Joshua did overtake the majority of the Promised Land, which consisted east and west of the Sea of Galilee and east and west from the Dead Sea and all the way south of the Negeb. The land was overrun slowly in order to acquire a cultivated land. But, although the majority of the land was possessed by the children of Israel, the children of Israel did not remove all of the inhabitants of the land as they were commissioned to do by Moses before he died. Instead, they became complacent with the inheritance they received.

We are told,

"23 Joshua took the whole land, according to all that the LORD said unto Moses; and Joshua gave it for an inheritance unto Israel according to their divisions by their tribes. And the land rested from war." Joshua 11:23

Not too many years after the children of Israel had settled in the Promised Land, Joshua in his old age decided to speak to the children of Israel one more time because he observed that the children of Israel were gradually abandoning Christ the LORD God of Israel. He summoned the Levi priests to bring the Ark of the Covenant from Shiloh to Mount Ebo, which was near Shechem. And he called the leaders of Israel and all the people of Israel to meet him there. Joshua left his home at Timnathserah and went near Shechem to speak to the people.

Looking down from below the knee of Mount

Crossing the Jordan River

Ebo, Joshua said unto the people,

> "2 Thus saith the LORD God of Israel, Your fathers dwelt on the other side of the flood in old time, even Terah, the father of Abraham, and the father of Nachor: and they served other gods. 3 And I took your father Abraham from the other side of the flood, and led him throughout all the land of Canaan, and multiplied his seed [offspring], and gave him Isaac. 4 And I gave unto Isaac Jacob and Esau: and I gave unto Esau mount Seir, to possess it; but Jacob and his children went down into Egypt.

> "5 I sent Moses also and Aaron, and I plagued Egypt, according to that which I did among them: and afterward I brought you out. 6 And I brought your fathers out of Egypt: and ye [all of you] came unto the sea; and the Egyptians pursued after your fathers with chariots and horsemen unto the Red sea.

> "7 And when they cried unto the LORD, He put darkness between you and the Egyptians, and brought the sea upon them, and covered them; and your eyes have seen what I have done in Egypt: and ye dwelt in the wilderness a long season. 8 And I brought you into the land of the Amorites, which dwelt on the other side Jordan; and they fought with you: and I gave them into your hand, that ye might possess their land; and I destroyed them from before you.

Crossing the Jordan River

"9 Then Balak the son of Zippor, king of Moab, arose and warred against Israel, and sent and called Balaam the son of Beor to curse you [See Numbers 22 and onward for the full details]: 10 But I would not hearken unto Balaam; therefore he blessed you still: so I delivered you out of his hand.

"11 And ye went over Jordan, and came unto Jericho: and the men of Jericho fought against you, the Amorites and the Perizzites, and the Canaanites, and the Hittites, and the Girgashites, the Hivites, and the Jebusites; and I delivered them into your hand. 12 And I sent the hornet before you, which drave them out from before you, even the two kings of the Amorites; but not with thy sword, nor with thy bow.

"13 And I have given you a land for which ye [all of you] did not labour, and cities which ye built not, and ye dwell in them; of the vineyards and oliveyards which ye planted not do ye eat. 14 Now therefore fear the LORD, and serve Him in sincerity and in truth: and put away the gods which your fathers served on the other side of the flood, and in Egypt; and serve ye the LORD.

"15 And if it seem evil unto you to serve the LORD, choose you this day whom ye will serve; whether the gods which your fathers served that were on the other side of the flood, or the gods of the Amorites, in whose land ye dwell: but as for me and my house, we will

Crossing the Jordan River

serve the LORD.

"16 And the people answered and said, God forbid that we should forsake the LORD, to serve other gods."

But, Joshua reminded the children of Israel that the LORD knows the secrets of their hearts; therefore,

"19 Joshua said unto the people, Ye cannot serve the LORD: for He is an holy God; He is a jealous God; He will not forgive your transgressions nor your sins. 20 If ye forsake the LORD, and serve strange gods, then He will turn and do you hurt, and consume you, after that He hath done you good. 21 And the people said unto Joshua, Nay; but we will serve the LORD. 22 And Joshua said unto the people, Ye are witnesses against yourselves that ye have chosen you the LORD, to serve Him. And they said, We are witnesses.

"23 Now therefore put away, said he, the strange gods which are among you, and incline your heart unto the LORD God of Israel.

"24 And the people said unto Joshua. The LORD our God will we serve, and His voice will we obey.

"25 So Joshua made a covenant with the people that day, and set them a statute and an ordinance in Shechem. 26 And Joshua wrote these words in the book

Crossing the Jordan River

of the law of God, and took a great stone, and set it up there under an oak, that was by the sanctuary of the LORD. 27 And Joshua said unto all the people, Behold, this stone shall be a witness unto us; for it hath heard all the words of the LORD which He spake unto us: it shall be therefore a witness unto you, lest ye deny your God. 28 So Joshua let the people depart, every man unto his inheritance. 29 And it came to pass after these things, that Joshua the son of Nun, the servant of the LORD, died, being an hundred and ten years old. 30 And they buried him in the border of his inheritance in Timnathserah, which is in mount Ephraim, on the north side of the hill of Gaash" (Joshua 24:2-16, 19-30).

As we have read, in the foregoing presentation, the children of Israel were admonished to go and posses the Promised Land, early in their second year of their journey, when they were in Kadesh-barnea. But since they refused to go in at that time to possess the Promised Land, in His mercy, Christ the LORD granted the children of Israel, as per their request, to live their lives in the wilderness. As a reminder of their refusal to go and possess the Promised Land, their forty days of spying in the Promised Land turned into forty years of wandering in the wilderness. Even though they abandoned the LORD God of Israel, at that time, in His compassion, God the Christ did not leave them; He stayed with them, fed them, protected them, and led them to greener pastures, in order to feed their animals.

But, on the fortieth year, again, the children of Israel were told to go and possess the Promised Land. This time, they obeyed the voice of the LORD and went from the wilderness of Paran, crossed the Brook Zered, and entered into the east side of the Dead Sea. Under

In the Promised Land

the command of Moses, the children of Israel overthrew the kings who opposed them, from the most southern tip of the Dead Sea, and all the way to the northern part of the Sea of Galilee. And on their forty-first year of their journey from the fields of Raamses, after the death of Moses, under the leadership of Joshua, the children of Israel crossed the River Jordan and went west to a place called Gilgal.

There at Gilgal, the children of Israel pitched their tents. There at Gilgal, the children of Israel were circumcised and celebrated the Passover. And after they celebrated the Passover, the manna stopped coming down the following day. From there onward, the children of Israel had to provide for themselves and for their livestock. And from Gilgal, under the guidance of Christ the LORD of hosts, and under the leadership of Joshua, the children of Israel prepared to remove the inhabitants of Canaan and made ready to divide their inheritance.

In the Promised Land

During the leadership of Joshua, in the Promised Land, the children of Israel worshiped Christ the God of Israel who resided in "the most holy place" of His Sanctuary in a place called "Shiloh" (1 Samuel 1:1-3).

In the Promised Land

In fact, they continued to worship the LORD God of Israel in "Shiloh," even after Joshua's death, at the age of 110. One of the reasons why the children of Israel continued to worship Christ the LORD God of Israel was because there were few dedicated individuals, who were contemporaries to Joshua; it was those individuals who kept the children of Israel on the side of Christ the LORD their God.

The record tells us, after their meeting in Shechem,

> "6 when Joshua had let the people go, the children of Israel went every man unto his inheritance to possess the land. 7 And the people served the LORD all the days of Joshua, and all the day of the elders that outlived Joshua, who had seen all the great works of the LORD, that He did for Israel" (Judges 2:6, 7).

But when the elders who outlived Joshua passed away, the children of Israel began to be attracted into the heathen practices by which they were surrounded. By allowing to be enticed into the heathen practices, the children of Israel gradually departed from Christ the LORD their God and chose to serve the pagan gods of the other nations.

If you recall, the children of Israel were told by Moses, not to,

> "24 bow down to their gods, nor serve them, nor do after their works: but thou [you] shalt utterly overthrow them, and quite break down their images, 25 And ye [all of you] shall serve the

In the Promised Land

> LORD your God, and He shall bless thy [your] bread, and thy water; and I will take sickness away from the midst of thee [you]."

And even more emphatically, the children of Israel were told,

> "32 Thou [you] shall make no covenant with them [heathens], nor with their gods" (Exodus 23:24, 25, 32).

The above message was repeated to the children of Israel on numerous occasions, as a reminder of their task, which lay before them. The command was that the children of Israel were to totally eradicate the inhabitants of Canaan, if the Canaanites did not want to leave or join the camp of Israel. But the children of Israel became complacent in their ways. After they received their inheritance, they did not totally drive their enemies out of their land as they were admonished. Therefore, the new generation became engrossed with the heathen practices and departed from Christ the LORD their God who dwelt in His Sanctuary, in a place called "Shiloh."

We are told; the new generation, "10 knew not the LORD, nor yet the works which He had done for Israel. 11 And the children of Israel did evil in the sight of the LORD, and served Baalim; 12 And they forsook the LORD God of their fathers, which brought them out of the land of Egypt, and followed other gods, of the gods of the people that were round about them, and bowed themselves unto them, and provoked the LORD to anger. 13 And they forsook the LORD, and served

Christ's Sovereignty .... By: Philip Mitanidis
In the Promised Land

Baal and Ashtaroth. 14 And the anger of the LORD was hot against Israel, and He delivered them into the hands of spoilers that spoiled them, and He sold them into the hands of their enemies round about, so that they could not any longer stand before their enemies. 15 Whithersoever they went out, the hand of the LORD was against them for evil, as the LORD had said, and as the LORD had sworn unto them: and they were greatly distressed. 16 Nevertheless the LORD raised up judges, which delivered them out of the hand of those that spoiled them. 17 And yet they would not hearken unto their judges, but they went a whoring after other gods, and bowed themselves unto them: they turned quickly out of the way which their fathers walked in, obeying the commandments of the LORD; but they did not so. 18 And when the LORD raised them up judges, then the LORD was with the judge, and delivered them out of the hand of their enemies all the days of the judge: for it repented the LORD because of their groanings by reason of them that oppressed them and vexed them.

> "19 And it came to pass, when the judge was dead, that they returned, and corrupted themselves more than their fathers, in following other gods to serve them, and to bow down unto them; they ceased not from their own doings, nor from their stubborn way. 20 And the anger of the LORD was hot against Israel; and He said, Because that this people hath transgressed My covenant which I commanded their fathers, and have not hearkened unto My voice;
>
> "21 I also will not henceforth

In the Promised Land

drive out any from before them of the nations which Joshua left when he died:

"22 That through them I may prove Israel, whether they will keep the way of the LORD to walk therein, as their fathers did keep it, or not.

"23 Therefore the LORD left those nations, without driving them out hastily; neither delivered He them into the hand of Joshua" (Judges 2:10-23).

What is outlined in the above verses is a simple fact that the children of Israel did not stay the course during the time period of the judges. They kept falling into apostasy. And the reason the children of Israel kept falling into apostasy was due to the fact that the children of Israel were lured into evil entrapments, which their pagan enemy delighted in. Consequently, the children of Israel, after while, preferred to engage in evil acts, and began to worshiped the statutes of Baal and Ashtaroth. And if I may add, the children of Israel chose to worship Baal and Ashtaroth because these gods allowed the children of Israel to live their lives in evil debase forms, which at the end became their detriment. I say that it became their detriment because satanic agencies did not want the children of Israel to go back to Christ the LORD God of their fathers and continue to promote the plan of salvation to the surrounding nations. Therefore, Satan and his evil

In the Promised Land

angels were bent on luring the children of Israel into deeper sensual evil acts, in order to destroy them. And when the children of Israel engrossed themselves by worshiping Baal and Ashtaroth, satanic agencies made their life a living hell; but Christ the LORD in His mercy kept an eye on His stray children. And, as the record reveals, He went and rescued them from their adversary the devil, when they did call upon Him.

In fact, if you continue to read the book of the judges, you will find that it gives us a glimpse how the children of Israel would depart from the LORD and live a sinful life; and when they ran into perilous times, they went back to their LORD God for safety.

It should be noted; Christ the LORD God of Israel, as the record reveals, did not abandon the children of Israel, even though they had left Him on numerous times.

It also appears from the record, as long as the children of Israel had a strong leader who worshiped Christ the LORD God of Israel, the children of Israel would follow their leader. But, if their leader veered off and chose to worship the pagan gods, and pagan practices, the majority of the children of Israel would also do the same. Although the children of Israel had the Torah in their possession, and it was read before the people, it did not mean very much to some who saw their leaders breaking the Covenant and influencing others to do the same; especially when there was no one to tell them not to depart from the LORD and not to live their lives in sin. Thus when the leaders of Israel entered in league with their pagan enemy, so did many of the children of Israel.

Here is a glimpse how the children of Israel,

In the Promised Land

during the time of the judges, would leave the LORD and continue to live in sin for a number of years; and then, come back to Him when satanic agencies used and oppressed them. They would stay with the LORD for few years; then, they would start sinning again for number of years. This oscillation of leaving Christ the LORD and coming back to Christ the LORD, it appears from the record that the children of Israel continued even beyond the reign of the judges.

Early during the time period of the judges, we are told that

> "5 the children of Israel dwelt among the Canaanites, Hittites, and Amorites, and Perizzites, and Hivites, and Jebusites: 6 And they took their daughters to be their wives, and gave their daughters to their sons, and served their gods. 7 And the children of Israel did evil in the sight of the LORD, and forgat the LORD their God, and served Baalim and the groves" (Judges 3:5-7).

According to verse eight, the children of Israel served other gods for eight years before they came to a conclusion that it is better to serve Christ the LORD God of Israel than to serve evil. When they realized that their tragic lives were becoming worse, they finally called upon Christ the LORD to save them from their ordeal. And He did. He sent a deliverer "9 to the children of Israel, who delivered them, even Othniel the son of Kenaz, Caleb's younger brother" (Judges 3:9).

After the LORD delivered the children of Israel, they remained with Christ the LORD for forty years;

In the Promised Land

and then, they plunged themselves into immoral acts again by serving other gods. This time they served "14 Eglon the king of Moab eighteen years" before they decided to come back to Christ the LORD God of their fathers. This time, when the children of Israel repented, they managed to stay with Christ the LORD for "30 fourscore years" (eighty years) before they went and did evil in the sight of the LORD.

"31 And after him [Ehud] was Shamgar the son of Anath, which slew of the Philistines six hundred men with an ox goad: and he also delivered Israel" (Judges 3:14, 30, 31).

"1 AND the children of Israel again did evil in the sight of the LORD, when Ehud was dead. 2 And the LORD sold them into the hand of Jabin king of Canaan, that reigned in Hazor; the captain of whose host was Sisera, which dwelt in Harosheth of the Gentiles. 3 And the children of Israel cried unto the LORD: for he had nine hundred chariots of iron; and twenty years he mightily oppressed the children of Israel" (Judges 4:1-3).

When the children of Israel repented and sought after Christ the LORD, He sent Deborah, a prophetess, and Barak to deliver the children of Israel from their evil oppression. Deborah told Barak to go and eliminate their enemy, but he said to her "I want you to go with me." Deborah agreed to go with him, but at the same time, Deborah told Barak that he was not going to receive the glory when he wins the war. She told him that a woman was going to receive the honor. Nonetheless, Deborah did go with Barak and his ten thousand men of war to Kedesh-naphtali.

When Sisera found out that Barak had gone up

In the Promised Land

to Mount Tabor, he gathered his nine hundred chariots, foot soldiers from Harosheth, and made ready to go to war with Barak.

Knowing that Sisera was ready to fight the children of Israel, Christ the LORD told Deborah to tell Barak to go down from the mountain and engage the battle with Sisera. After Barak demolished Sisera's army, Sisera fled by running away from them on foot to a tent, which was owned by Heber's wife Jael. When he saw her in the tent, he sought refuge there. He went in her tent and said unto her,

> "19 Give me, I pray thee, a little water to drink; for I am thirsty. And she opened a bottle of milk, and gave him drink, and covered him. 20 Again he said unto her, Stand in the door of the tent, and it shall be, when any man doth come and enquire of thee [you], and say, Is there any man here? that thou [you] shalt say, No" (Judges 4:19, 20).

She agreed.

And when Sisera was at ease with her watch, he relaxed while he lay comfortably at rest. When Jael saw him resting, she cautiously moved about getting a large spike and a hammer. When she gathered the iron spike and the hammer into her hands, she stealthily moved towards Sisera and drove the large iron spike right into his temples, by hammering it vigorously into his skull. After a short struggle to stop the blows into his head, Sisera died.

Meanwhile Barak continued to pursue Sisera, and he vowed to find him. In his search, he came across

In the Promised Land

the tent of Jael. And when Jael saw Barak, she called him over and said to him, "22 Come, and I will shew thee the man whom thou [you] seekest. And when he came into her tent, behold, Sisera lay dead, and the nail was in his temples. 23 So God subdued on that day Jabin the king of Canaan before the children of Israel" (Judges 4:22, 23).

After that, the children of Israel prospered and had a rest for forty years from their enemies. But again, "1 the children of Israel did evil in the sight of the LORD: and the LORD delivered them into the hand of Midian seven years. 2 And the hand of Midian prevailed against Israel: and because of the Midianites the children of Israel made them the dens which are in the mountains, and caves, and strongholds. 3 And so it was, when Israel had sown, that the Midianites came up, and the Amalekites, and the children of the east, even they came up against them; 4 And they encamped against them, and destroyed the increase of the earth, till thou come unto Gaza, and left no sustenance for Israel, neither sheep, nor ox, nor ass. 5 For they came up with their cattle and their tents, and they came as grasshoppers for multitude; for both they and their camels were without number: and they entered into the land to destroy it. 6 And Israel was greatly impoverished because of the Midianites; and the children of Israel cried unto the LORD. 7 And it came to pass, when the children of Israel cried unto the LORD because of the Midianites.

"8 That the LORD sent a prophet unto the children of Israel, which said unto hem, Thus saith the LORD God of Israel, I brought you up from Egypt, and brought you forth out of the house of bondage; 9 And I

In the Promised Land

delivered you out of the hand of the Egyptians, and out of the hand of all that oppressed you, and drave them out from before you, and gave you their land; 10 And I said unto you, I am the LORD your God; fear not the gods of the Amorites, in whose land ye dwell: but ye have not obeyed My voice" (Judges 6:1-10).

Yes the children of Israel did not obey Christ the LORD; they chose to serve the heathen gods. But in His mercy Christ the LORD came to their rescue when they called upon Him. The LORD sent a man called Gideon to deliver the children of Israel from the Midianites. But Gideon, like many other Israelites, wondered if Christ the LORD was with them.

> "13 why then" he asked "is all this befallen us? and where be are all His miracles which our fathers told us of, saying, Did not the LORD bring us up from Egypt? but now the LORD hath forsaken us, and delivered us into the hands of the Midianites" (Judges 6:13).

Although Gideon was skeptical, Christ the LORD assured him that he will deliver the Midianites into his hands and destroy them, if he would only place his trust in the LORD. Gideon accepted the challenge. He gathered three hundred men as the LORD directed him and went to battle with the Midianites. "28 Thus was Midian subdued before the children of Israel, so that they lifted up their heads no more. And the country was in quietness forty years in the days of Gideon" (Judges 8:28).

But, as their appetite for evil acts persisted, and their desire to pursue evil debased acts ballooned in their lives, again, they forsook Christ the LORD their God who delivered them from the ravages of the Midianites. The record says,

> "33 And it came to pass, as soon as Gideon was dead, that the children of Israel turned again, and went a whoring after Baalim, and made Baalberith their god. 34 And the children of Israel remembered not the LORD their God, who had delivered them out of the hands of all their enemies on every side: 35 Neither shewed they kindness to the house of Jerubbaal, namely, Gideon, according to all the goodness which he had shewed unto Israel" (Judges 8:33-35).

As you have read in the above verses, you can see the children of Israel plunge themselves into idolatry and debase sinful acts again and again. They chose to serve other gods because many of their leaders did not restrain them. Nonetheless, if you were to continue to read the book of the judges, you will notice that the apostasy and repentance of the children of Israel continued well beyond the time period of the judges. Somehow, the children of Israel refused to stay with Christ the LORD God of their fathers perpetually. Their history, from the time they came out of Egypt and into the Promised Land, reveals that they did not remain with Christ the LORD their God all the time. In fact, as per their own historical record, the children of Israel have remained in apostasy in a longer period of time than they have remained loyal to Christ the LORD God of Israel.

Having said that, the above statement does not

In the Promised Land

mean that all of the children of Israel abandoned the LORD their God during their apostasy; they did not. There were always individuals who remained loyal to the LORD God of Israel. That fact is evident because from those loyal individuals, the LORD God of Abraham chose and sent spokesmen on His behalf to direct the children of Israel back to Himself.

It should further be apparent; the reason the children of Israel continued in their apostasy was due to two factors. One, the children of Israel did not remove all of the heathens from the Promised Land, as they were admonished to do. Two, when the children of Israel were told not to mingle or interact with the heathen practices, they refused to obey the voice of Christ the LORD their God. Because the children of Israel refused to obey and to worship Christ the LORD God of their fathers, and refused to clear all of the inhabitants off the Promised Land, as they were told by Moses, Christ the LORD left a number of heathen kings in the Promised Land as a witness to their disobedience.

These kings are as follows: "3 Namely, the five lords of the Philistines, and all the Canaanites, and the Sidonians, and the Hivites that dwelt in mount Lebanon, from mount Baalhermon unto the entering in of Hamath. 4 And they were to prove Israel by them, to know whether they would hearken unto the commandments of the LORD, which He commanded their fathers by the hand of Moses" (Judges 3:3, 4).

Although Christ the LORD of hosts the God of Israel did prove the children of Israel, while they were living in the Promised Land, many times, as the record shows, they fell from the grace of God the Christ and went on whoring with the heathen nations in the sight

Claiming Sovereignty

of the LORD to do evil to others and to themselves.

But, in His mercy, as the inspired Scriptures reveal, Christ the LORD God of Abraham and of Israel patiently continued to dwell in His Sanctuary in Shiloh, until near the end of the judges. At that time, He abandoned His Sanctuary because the Levi priests and the children of Israel polluted the Sanctuary so badly that it caused Christ the LORD God of Israel to abandon His dwelling place amongst the tribe of Ephraim. Although He abandoned His Sanctuary, which was pitched in "Shiloh," He did not abandon the children of Israel. He continued to reach out to them and waited for their return with open arms; and that welcome is still there today.

CLAIMING SOVEREIGNTY

Previous, it was aptly revealed and identified that Jesus Christ the LORD of hosts is the LORD God of "Abraham and of the children of Israel. And, it was also revealed that there are three Individuals in the Godhead by the names of "God the Christ," "God the Father," and "God the Holy Ghost" who is often

Claiming Sovereignty

referred to, by the name of "The Holy Spirit," and sometimes by the name of "Spirit." And that being a Scriptural fact, why is Jesus Christ the LORD of hosts saying,

> "5 there is no God beside Me" (Isaiah 44:5),

when knowingly, there are two other Gods" in existence who work in Chrisr's administration (1 Corinthians 12:5) and go by the character names of "God the Father" and God the Holy Ghost?

Simplistically, He does because He is the Sovereign God of His universe and of "all things," which He created for Himself and by Himself. Please let the prophet of the LORD emphasize the Scriptural fact that "16 all things were created by Him [Christ], and for Him [Christ]," "17 and by Him [Christ] all things consist." Colossians 1:16, 17

Did you notice; Apostle Paul says, "all things" were created "by Him" (Christ) and "for Him" (Christ). Those are not my words, they are Apostle Paul's words. As a result, "all things were not created for someone else or by someone else. They were created for Christ and by Christ. Therefore, Christ the LORD of hosts is the owner and Sovereign God of "all things," which He created for Himself.

As per the Old and New testaments, Jesus Christ the LORD God of Abraham and of Israel created "all things," the universe, "all things" in the universe, and outside of the universe, as you have read, by Himself and for Himself.

To further confirm the fact that "all things" were

Christ's Sovereignty.......... *By: Philip Mitanidis*

Claiming Sovereignty

created for Christ and by Christ, here are a handful of Bible references, which clearly state that Christ the LORD of hosts created "all things" for Himself and by Himself; and therefore making Him the sole Creator, and owner of "all things." And as a result, He is the supreme Sovereign God of the universe and of the third heaven.

Apostle Paul writes,

"16 For by Him [Christ] were all things created, that are in heaven, and that are in earth, visible and invisible, whether they be thrones, or dominions, or principalities, or powers: all things were created by Him [Christ], and for Him [Christ]:

"17 And He is before all things, and by Him [Christ] all things consist." Colossians 1:16, 17

Here are the above verses in the Greek text. They read as follows,

"16 επειδη δι' [by] αυτου εκτισθησαν τα παντα, τα εν τοις ουρανοις και τα επι της γης, τα ορατα και τα αορατα, ειτε θρονοι, ειτε κυριοτητες, ειτε αρχαι, ειτε εξουσιαι, τα παντα δι' [by] αυτου και εις [for] αυτον εκτισθησαν.

"17 και αυτος ειναι προ παντων, και τα παντα συντηρουνται δι' [by] αυτου." Κολοσσαεις 1:16, 17   Βιβλικη Εταιρεια   Colossians 1:16, 17

Claiming Sovereignty

Although the above Greek text clearly states, "all things were created by Him [Christ], and for Him [Christ]," some would argue that the above verses do not say, Christ created "all things" by Himself and for Himself. They say, "God the Father" created "all things" "through" Christ. And yet, if you were to look at the above two verses in the (OKJV) and the Greek text, you will notice, first of all, the word "through" does not exist in these verses. Secondly, the words "God the Father" do not exist in the above verses. Consequently, we can conclude that these verses in your Bible, which state, somebody created the "all things" "through" Jesus Christ, are mistranslated.

According to the above two verses, which are written by Apostle Paul, we can see that there are no discrepancies in the translation of the Greek word "δι'" (by). The translators of the (OKJV) of the Bible used the word "by" correctly, whenever the Greek word "δι'" appears in these creation verses. But, it should be noticed, many translators have translated the word "δι'" to read "through," which is one hundred percent incorrect. The word "δι'" in the Greek text reads "by." And it should be further observed; if we were to embrace the uninspired word "through" in these verses, then we will create a total disaster upon Scripture because nowhere in the Old Testament creation verses the uninspired word "through" is used. And, if we use it, then we will cause the New Testament to contradict the Old Testament.

Do you really want to go down that road?

Do you vindictively want to add and delete words from Christ's Gospel?

If you do, remember, there are some severe

Claiming Sovereignty

warnings throughout the Bible to those individuals who choose to add, alter, or to delete the words of the prophets. One of the warnings reads as follows:

> "8 But though we, or an angel from heaven, preach any other gospel unto you than that which we have preached unto you, let him be accursed.
>
> "9 As we said before, so say I now again, If any man preach any other gospel unto you than that ye [all of you] have received, let him be accursed." Galatians 1:8, 9

Nonetheless, Apostle Paul writes, "For by Him [Christ] were all things created." And again Apostle Paul says, "all things were created by Him [Christ], and for Him [Christ]."

And in verse seventeen, Apostle Paul says, "and by Him [Christ] all things consist." Colossians 1:17

These two verses (Colossian 1:16, 17), as you probably have noticed, say almost the same thing as the verse that is found in Romans 11:36.

The verse in the Greek text reads,

> "36 Επειδη εξ [of] αυτου [Him], και δι' [by] αυτου [Him], και εις [for] αυτου [Him], ειναι τα παντα αυτω η δοξα εις τους αιωνας. Αμην." Προς Ρωμαιους 11:36 Βιβλικη Εταιρεια Romans 11:36

In Romans eleven thirty-six Apostle Paul says, "all things" came into existence "of Him" (Christ).

Claiming Sovereignty

"all things" were created "by Him" (Christ). And the creation was created "for Him" (Christ).

Did you notice the similar statements that are made by Apostle Paul in Colossians 1:16, 17. He says, "all things were created by Him [Christ], and for Him [Christ]." And the apostle adds, "by Him [Christ] all things consist."

By reading the above verses, they do not leave any room for doubt that it was Christ who created "all things" out of Himself, by Himself, and for Himself. Thus, "all things" are "of Him" (εξ αυτου), and "by Him" (δι' αυτου), and "for Him" (εις αυτου). Romans 11:36

Consequently, as per the above verses, the sole Creator of "all things" is Christ the "LORD of hosts," the "God of Israel" by whom "all things consist" (Colossians 1:17). The reason they "all consist" by Christ the owner of "all things" is due to the fact that He is the sole Creator and sustainer.

That is why you cannot find, in the Hebrew text or in the Greek text a co-creator involved with Jesus Christ the LORD anywhere in the entire Bible.

And since we cannot find a co-creator with Christ the LORD, anywhere in the entire sixty-six books of the Bible, we can agree with Jesus Christ the LORD of hosts when He says that He created "all things alone" and as He says, "by My self."

Here is one of the reference:

> "24 I am the LORD that maketh all things; that stretcheth forth the heavens alone; that spreadeth abroad the earth by Myself" (Isaiah 44:24).

Claiming Sovereignty

Did you hear that?

Christ the LORD of hosts plainly states that He created "all things," "alone," and as He has said, He created "all things" "by Myself." Therefore there is no one else involved in the creation of "all things" with Christ the LORD God of Israel. He did not need any help, advice, power, wisdom, etc., etc., to create everything that is in the universe and outside of the universe. He created "all thing" by the word of His mouth. He spake and it was done.

> "6 By the word of the LORD were the heavens made; and all the host of them by the breath of His mouth.
>
> "7 He gathereth the waters of the sea together as an heap: He layeth up the depth in storehouses. 8 Let all the earth fear the LORD: let all the inhabitants of the world stand in awe of Him.
>
> "9 For He spake, and it was done; He commanded, and it stood fast." Psalms 33:6-9

As you have observed, the Psalmist, like Apostle Paul, sights similar attributes to Christ "the LORD God of Israel" and Creator of "all things." They are "power," "wisdom," "knowledge," and "judgment." And the prophet of the LORD further states, "how unsearchable are...His ways"? And then, he asks a number of serious questions for you and for me to consider.

He asks,

Claiming Sovereignty

> "₃₄ For who hath known the mind of the LORD? or who hath been His counsellor?
>
> "₃₅ Or who hath first given to Him, and it shall be recompensed unto Him again? Romans 11:33-35

Very good questions don't you think?
So! Who knows the mind of Christ the Creator the "God of Israel"?

Or, who has been Christ's counsellor, helper, or a guide to guide Him in the creation of the universe and outside of the universe?

Or, who has given Christ the LORD of hosts anything or something that He has to compensate, reimburse, repay, be indebted, or do favors for?

Obviously to no one because,

> "₃₆ For "of Him" [εξ αυτου], and "by Him" [δι' αυτου], and "for Him" [εις αυτου] are all things: to whom be glory for ever. Amen." Roman 11:36 (Translation is mine.)

As you have read in the above verses, Apostle Paul agrees with the Old Testament creation verses that no one understands the mind of Christ the LORD of hosts, or gave Christ "the God of Israel" any advice, knowledge, wisdom, understanding, power, or helped Him, in some way, in order to create the universe and every thing that is in it and outside of it.

Jeremiah adds,

Claiming Sovereignty

> "12 He hath made the earth by His power, He hath established the world by His wisdom, and hath stretched out the heavens by His discretion" (Jeremiah 10:12).

Did you notice the word "discretion"?

Jeremiah the prophet of the LORD of hosts (v.16) says, He "stretched out the heavens by His discretion" (Jeremiah 10:12). And he also adds, He hath established "the world by His wisdom."

And, since Christ created "all things" by His "discretion" and by "His wisdom" that means no one has given Christ the "God of Israel" anything or helped Him, at any time, during the creation of "all things." Therefore, He does not have to compensate or give back anything to anyone.

And the reason why Christ "the LORD of hosts" "the God of Israel" does not have to repay anyone is due to the fact that "of Him, and by Him, and for Him, are all things."

Here is the reference,

> "36 For of Him, and by [δι'] Him, and for Him, are all things: to whom be glory for ever. Amen." Roman 11:36 (Translation is mine.)

And, here is the above verse in the Greek text, which confirms the fact that "all things" are "of Him" (Christ), "by [δι'] Him" (Christ), and "for Him" (Christ); it reads as follows,

Christ's Sovereignty………. *By: Philip Mitanidis*
Claiming Sovereignty

"36 Επειδη εξ [of] αυτου [Him], και δι' [by] αυτου [Him], και εις [for] αυτου [Him], ειναι τα παντα αυτω η δοξα εις τους αιωνας. Αμην." Προς Ρωμαιους 11:36 Βιβλικη Εταιρεια Romans 11:36

As you have read in the above verse, "all things" are "of Him" (Christ) or "out of Him" (Christ). The Greek text reads, "εξ αυτου" (of Him). That means "all things" in the universe, the universe, and outside of the universe, all came into existence "of Him" (εξ αυτου) Christ the LORD of hosts. As per v.36, "all things" did not come into existence from someone else.

Furthermore, concerning the "all things," it should be noted that the verse in the (OKJV) (Romans 11:36), contrary to the Greek text says that "all things" came into existence "through Him" (Christ). It, like many mistranslated Bibles that are in the marketplace today, reads "through Him." But, how can "all things" come "through Him" (Christ), when the previous statement in v.36 clearly says, "all things" came out "of Him" ("εξ αυτου"), from Him (Christ), or "of Him" (Christ), if you like? That is a total contradictory presentation by the (OKJV) of the Bible. And, if I may add, by the majority of the New Testament Bibles that are translated from the Greek to English.

Therefore let us look at the Greek text again and then compare it to the (OKJV) of the Bible to see if the Greek text has been translated correctly into English to read "by."

The Greek text reads,

Claiming Sovereignty

"36 Επειδη εξ αυτου, και δι' [by] αυτου, και εις αυτου, ειναι τα παντα αυτω η δοξα εις τους αιωνας. Αμην." Προς Ρωμαιους 11:36 Βιβλικη Εταιρεια Romans 11:36

The Greek text above reads correctly "δι' [by] αυτου" (by Him). And here is the verse in the (OKJV). It reads incorrectly, "through Him."

"36 For of Him, and through Him, and to Him, are all things: to whom be glory for ever. Amen." Roman 11:36

As you can readily see in the first line of verse thirty-six, in the Greek text, the Greek word "δι' " is present; and when it is translated into English, it will read "by." For that reason, I placed the word [by] in brackets next to the Greek word "δι' " to indicate the correct translation from Greek to English.

Therefore the verse in Romans 11:36 of the (OKJV) of the Bible should read, "all things" were created "by Him" Christ the LORD God of Israel.

Strangely, if I can say that, the translators of the (OKJV) of the Bible have translated the rest of the creation verses (John 1:3, 10; Colossians 1:16, 17) in the New Testament to read "by" whenever the Greek word "δι' " is used by the prophets of Christ the LORD of hosts, with the exception of Romans 11:36.

Why was Romans eleven thirty-six mistranslated in the (OKJV), when the rest of the creation verses are not, is a good question? Maybe it was a new batch of translators who arrived on the job

Claiming Sovereignty

one day, and by not consulting with the other creation verses, or questioned the other creation verses, caused the verse to be mistranslated? But the fact that the translators of the (OKJV) translated the Greek word "δι' " to read correctly "by" in the rest of the creation verses (John 1:3, 10; Colossians 1:16, 17), reveals that some of the translators of the (OKJV) of the Bible made a mistake in Romans 11:36.

But, to their credit, by using the correct translated word "by," in the rest of the creation verses that exist in the New Testament, they do not contradict the Old Testament creation verses. I say that they do not contradict the Old Testament creation verses because none of the creation verses in the Hebrew or in the Greek texts use the uninspired word "through" (δια μεσου or αναμασου) in any of the creation verses.

Therefore there is no contradiction or disagreement found in the following creation verses, John 1:3, 10; and with Colossians 1:16, 17. As per the Greek text, they all use the word "δι' " (by).

Unfortunately, for whatever reason the (OKJV) of the Bible in Romans 11:36 is mistranslated. But, since the Greek word "δι' " (by) does exist in the Greek text, we can safely use the word "by" to make the correction in Romans 11:36 to read "by [δι'] Him."

Thus, the verse in Romans eleven thirty-six will read as follows,

> "36 For of Him, and by [δι'] Him, and for Him, are all things: to whom be glory for ever. Amen." Roman 11:36 (OKJV corrected to read "by Him.")

Claiming Sovereignty

In addition, the above verse states that the "all things" that were created by Christ the LORD God of Israel, they were created "for Him."

Did you notice?

"All things" were created not only "by [δι'] Him" (Christ); but, they were also created "for Him" (Christ). That means "all things" were not created for someone else!

That is why Christ "the LORD of hosts," when referring to His creation of "all things," said,

> "15 All things that the Father hath are mine: therefore said I, that he shall take of mine, and shall shew it unto you."
> John 16:15

If the apostle's statement, rather statements "of Him," "for Him," and "by Him" (Romans 11:36 and Colossians 1:16, 17), and Christ's statement, "15 All things that the Father hath are mine" (John 16:15), come as a surprise to you, you should not despair because Christ the LORD of hosts and His prophets of old provide more support for His ownership and Sovereignty over "all things" throughout the Bible.

Nonetheless, as you can see, to avoid confusion as to who is the sole Creator of "all things," and to whom the "all things" belong to, Apostle Paul presents to us six predominant points. He says, "all things," are "of Him," and "by Him," and "for Him," and "by Him [Christ] all things consist" (Colossians 1:17), and "to whom." And in five of these references, the singular pronoun is used to point out to you and to me the fact that there is only one Creator who created "all things."

Claiming Sovereignty

The singular pronouns are, "of Him," "by Him," "for Him," (Romans 11:36), "by Him [Christ] all things consist" (Colossians 1:17), and "to whom."

Therefore, it should be noticed, there is no statement found in the Greek text, which says, somebody created "through" Christ.

And since there is no other God involved in the creation of "all things" with Christ the LORD of hosts, as per Scripture, Christ is the Sovereign God of "all things," which He created for Himself, by Himself, "alone," and as He says, "by Myself" (Isaiah 44:24).

Consequently, since Jesus Christ the LORD of hosts claims that He is the owner and Sovereign God of "all things," which He created, in our universe and outside of our universe, and that there is "no God beside Him," where does it leave God the Father and God the Holy Spirit, as we know them now in the New Testament?

To get our answer, first picture our universe and outside of our universe, before sin entered in them.

When we look outside of our universe, identified, as per Scripture, as the third heaven, we will see array of things, which wrap around our universe and stretches beyond our imagination. And there, in the white space, before our universe was created thirteen point eight billion years ago, and before angels and other beings were created, was God the Creator, better known in the New Testament by the name of Jesus Christ the LORD of hosts, standing in the midst of the white space. And, within that white space, there were two other Gods with Him. And these three Gods had

Claiming Sovereignty

amicable interaction with each other. What sports, games, amusements, or delights they created to pacify themselves is a good question? But one thing is for sure; at one point, Christ put a proposal before His two Associates (the two Gods). And that proposal was to create beings with free willed moral minds. But, that suggestion did not go too well with His two Associates because the plan was too risky. It would not only jeopardize the well being of every created being, but also it would risk Christ's own existence, as they know it. Therefore they turned down the proposal.

But, after considering the benefits and the risks of creating free willed moral beings, the possibility of sin entering in both realms, and the possibility of Christ loosing His own life in the process, Christ the Creator chose to take that risk and began to create diversified environments and free willed moral diversified beings to live in those environments.

Christ the Creator first created His throne. After the creation of His throne, He created the four beasts (angels) who have eyes at the front and at the back of their wings. And, these angels hover in the midst of the throne and round about the throne of Christ the LORD of hosts (Isaiah 6:1-5). Then Christ created the twenty-four elders who sit around the throne of God the Christ. And after the creation of the elders, Christ created the ecosystems for a variety of angels to live in the third heaven.

And after the host of heaven was created, Jesus Christ the LORD created our universe. According to the scientific community, if their calculations are correct, our universe is thirteen point eight billion years old. And in our universe, Christ the LORD created a variety

Christ's Sovereignty.......... *By: Philip Mitanidis*

Claiming Sovereignty

of habitats for the created beings to live in. And one small segment called the Milky Way, edged between two spokes of our galaxy, as per new studies, was formed four and a half billion years ago. And in that formation, Jesus Christ the LORD created the ecosystem for the human race. And according to the scientific community, a recent study states that the earth's ecosystem began to evolve four point two billion years ago. But, previous studies have shown that the earth's ecosystem took place about three billion years ago. And yet, according to new fossils found in Africa, if the scientific community's calculations are correct (archeologists), the human race began in full maturity about one point six million years ago. Therefore, I place the creation of man, birds, animals, fish, and woman at one point six million years ago because the man, woman, birds, animals, fish, and vegetation were created by Christ in full maturity; it did not take four point two billion years, or three billion years, or over three million years, as these theories suggest, for all of them to evolve into mature state.

All of these theories have a big problem because there is a gap between their starting point and the earth's starting point. As an example, as per one theory, since our Solar System and our earth formed four and a half billion years ago, and our sun and moon formed three billion years ago, the sun and the moon are 1.5 billion years younger that the earth.

How did the sun and moon form after our Solar System formed? How did they get here? Did they just pop into our Solar System out of nowhere? This scenario sounds more like what Christ did during the creation of the ecosystem on earth. As per the Genesis

Claiming Sovereignty

account, Christ created the ecosystem first and then He created on the fourth day the sun and the moon; and on the sixth day He created man and woman.

Nonetheless, after the ecosystem on the earth was completed, Christ the Creator of "all things" created man and woman and placed them on earth to live in, and told them to multiply and fill the earth with their offspring.

But, at one point, pride entered in one of the commanding angels by the name of Lucifer, and sought to set a throne above Christ's throne, in order to be worshipped by all that Christ the LORD had created. Christ asked Lucifer to reconsider his actions and repent. But because of his pride, he became delusional, thinking that he would be more powerful than Christ because sin would not have any remorse or restrain upon all that he does. Therefore he went everywhere to deceive as many individuals as he could in order to set up his throne. And one of those individuals, whom he tempted, was Eve.

Eve, when she was tempted by Lucifer (Satan), chose to sin. And by sinning, she hoped that she would become a god; but quickly found out, to her horror, she was deceived. And when Adam learned about her sinful act, for whatever reason, he decided to sin also. If Adam was worried of being alone, Christ the Creator would have created another woman for Adam before Eve died or after Eve died. Why did he choose to sin and die with Eve?

After Eve and Adam sinned, and tasted the deception of sin, they repented. And when they repented, Christ the LORD spoke to them and explained the plan of Salvation for them and for their

Claiming Sovereignty

progeny. Christ would come in the flesh and die for their sins. And, if they remained loyal to Christ, they and their offspring would be resurrected and reinstated to eternal youthful life. And in order to save Adam, and Eve, and their children, Christ the LORD of hosts, before He came two thousand years ago in the flesh, to be born of a sinful woman (Galatians 4:4), He emptied Himself from all of His powers and became a mere man.

We are told:

> "5 Let this mind be in you, which was also in Christ Jesus: 6 Who, being in the form of God, thought it not robbery to be equal with God: 7 But made Himself of no reputation, and took upon Him the form of a servant, and was made in the likeness of men: 8 And being found in fashion as a man, He humbled Himself, and became obedient unto death, even the death of the cross." Philippians 2:5-8

In order for Christ the LORD to pay for the sins of the penitent sinners of the world, as the above verses state, He had to strip Himself from all powers and become a human being; otherwise, as a powerful Spirit being, His enemies would not be able to crucify Him.

And prior to taking upon Himself the form of a man, Christ left His administration in God the Father's keeping, while Christ came in the flesh, here on earth, on a mission to fulfill the Plan of Salvation. Therefore, as a man, Jesus Christ the LORD relied upon God the Father and upon God the Holy Spirit for strength,

Claiming Sovereignty

guidance, and protection, right up until He was crucified by the priests and leaders of the House of Judah (Jews). And when Christ was on earth in the flesh, He was recognized as the LORD God of Israel, the King of Israel, the Messiah, and as the Son of Christ's Associate (God the Father).

In passing, please note: God the Father was not a Father to Christ and neither was Christ a Son to God the Father prior to Christ's birth on earth. In agreement, Christ was to be "called" the Son of God when He came in the flesh.

Here are the references:

> "5 For unto which of the angels said he at any time, Thou [You] art my Son, this day have I begotten thee [You]? And again, I will be to Him a Father, and He shall be to me a Son?" Hebrews 1:5

And Gabriel, the angel, said to Mary, "31 And, behold, thou [you] shalt conceive in thy [you] womb, and bring forth a son, and

"shalt call His name JESUS. 32 He shall be great,

"and shall be called the Son of the Highest:

"and the Lord God shall give unto Him the throne of his father David" (Luke 1:31, 32).

As you have read in the above verses, Jesus Christ the LORD of hosts, after He stripped Himself

Claiming Sovereignty

from all of His powers and came in the flesh, He was to be "called the Son of the Highest [God the Father]." God the Father said, "I will be to Him a Father, and He shall be to me a Son?" (Hebrews 1:5).

God the Father makes the above statement because Jesus Christ the LORD is from everlasting to everlasting (Psalms 90:1, 2), He has no beginning or end. Therefore how can He possibly be a son to anyone, unless it is by an arrangement?

Nonetheless, when sin entered first in the third heaven, and later on earth, one third of the angels who sinned chose not to be saved, therefore they were cast down from the third heaven on planet earth to live amongst sinful men and women.

Here are the references:

> "7 And there was war in heaven: Michael and his angels fought against the dragon; and the dragon fought and his angels, 8 And prevailed not; neither was their place found any more in heaven.

> "9 And the great dragon was cast out, that old serpent, called the Devil, and Satan, which deceiveth the whole world: he was cast out into the earth, and his angels were cast out with him" (Revelation 12:7-9).

As you have read in the above verses, Lucifer (Satan) was cast down upon the earth with his unruly evil angels because he had nowhere else to go. Adam and Eve forfeited to Satan the dominion of the earth,

190   Christ's Sovereignty……... *By: Philip Mitanidis*
Claiming Sovereignty

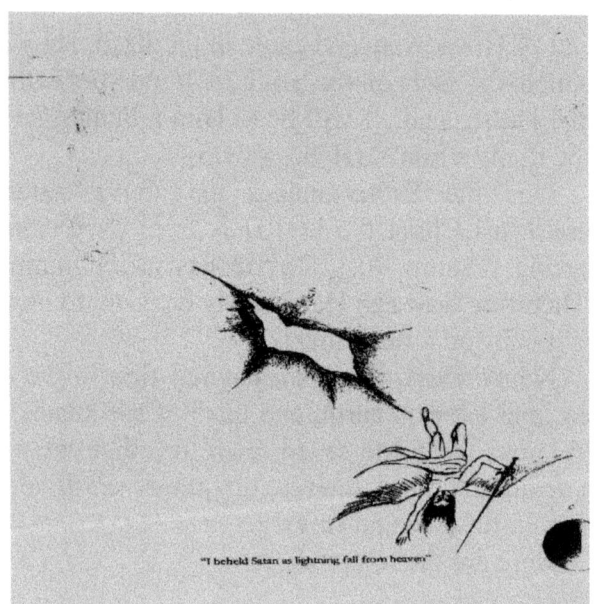
"I beheld Satan as lightning fall from heaven."

which was given to them by Christ; therefore, since Satan and his followers were given dominion over the earth by Adam, they were all cast down upon the earth to live.

Looking at the above scene, Jesus said,

> "18 And He [Christ] said unto them, I beheld Satan as lightning fall from heaven." Luke 10:18

And when the above evil events took place, Christ the LORD had to eradicate the evil that was created by the unrepentant angels and man, if He wanted to have a sinless universe? Consequently, as per Revelation 12:7-9, something horribly did go wrong (sin entered in both realms). Therefore, Christ the Creator of "all things," was responsible for the well

Christ's Sovereignty.......... *By: Philip Mitanidis*
Claiming Sovereignty

being of all He had created. And, as a responsible Creator, He had to come down to earth and pay the penalty for the sinners (Romans 6:23), if He wanted to save them and His Kingdom? Therefore, He came on planet earth in the form of a human being, in order to be crucified and save all of the individuals who wanted and want today to be saved in His Kingdom.

And once Jesus Christ died on Calvary's cross without sinning, the Plan of Salvation was complete. Now men and women before the cross and after the cross can be saved by Christ's grace because of His supreme sacrifice—if they want to? If they don't, they will hate Christ and His penitent sinners until such time they repent; and if they don't repent, they will die in their sins and be lost forever.

Nonetheless, the message is clear; we are told,

> "$_8$ But God commendeth his love toward us, in that, while we were yet sinners, Christ died for us.

> "$_9$ Much more then, being now justified by His blood, we shall be saved from wrath through Him." Romans 5:8, 9

After Christ's death, on Friday the 14th, the women came to the sepulcher on Sunday morning (the first day of the week), and found that Christ was not there; He had risen from the dead. Christ went to heaven temporary after His resurrection; and then came back to planet earth to expound the Scriptures to the apostles, which they did not understand; and to give them power, encouragement, and strength for their

Claiming Sovereignty

mission to spread Christ's Gospel to a perishing world. And when He finished His contact with the apostles, He went back to the third heaven. And when He arrived there, God the Father said to Christ the LORD, sit on my right hand until I make Your enemies Your footstool.

Here is the record:

> "1 A Psalm of David. The Lord said unto my LORD, Sit Thou [You] at my right hand, until I make thine [Your] enemies thy [Your] footstool" (Psalms 110:1).

To clarify the verse, it will read as follows:

> "1 A Psalm of David. The Lord [God the Father] said unto my LORD [Christ], Sit thou [You] at my right hand, until I make thine [Your] enemies thy [Your] footstool" (Psalms 110:1).

As you have read, after Christ was resurrected, Christ was to sit on the right hand of God the Father "until" such a time God the Father makes Christ's enemies His footstool.

And after God the Father puts all of Christ's enemies under Christ's feet, Christ is to come to planet earth with His holy angels and park themselves way up in the sky. And from there, Christ is to resurrect all of His penitent dead people from their watery and dusty graves. And when they come out of their graves, they and the penitent sinners that are alive will be taken to the third heaven.

Claiming Sovereignty

And there, the transition will take place between God the Christ and God the Father. God the Father is to give back or return, if you like, to Christ, Christ's throne (Isaiah 6:1-5) and "all things," which Christ had created.

God the Father will say to Christ the LORD of hosts,

> "₈ But unto the Son he [God the Father] saith, Thy [Your] throne, O God, is for ever and ever: a sceptre of righteousness is the sceptre of thy [Your] kingdom" (Hebrews 1:8).

"₂₄ Then cometh the end, when he shall have delivered up the kingdom to God [The Greek text reads "τω Θεω."], even the Father; when he shall have put down all rule and all authority and power.

> "₂₅ For he [God the Father] must reign, till he hath put all enemies under His [Christ's] feet" 1 Corinthians 15:24, 25

Since Christ has left His Kingdom in God the Father's keeping until all of Christ's enemies are put under Christ's feet, by God the Father; as per their agreement, God the Father,

> "₂₅ must reign, till he hath put all enemies under His [Christ's] feet" (1 Corinthians 15:25).

Claiming Sovereignty

And when God the Father puts "all enemies under His [Christ's] feet," then he has to return Christ's Kingdom (all things, which Christ had created) back to Christ. And when God the Father gives Christ's Kingdom (v.24) back to Christ, he is not legally responsible for it (v.27). Then Christ begins to reign again over His creation and over His administration (1 Corinthians 12:5). Thus Christ's Sovereignty will be recognized by every living being as it is recognized by God the Father (Hebrews 1:8; 1 Corinthians 15:25).

And in order not to exclude God the Father from Christ's reign over "all things," Christ inturn subjects everything that was subjected to Him back to God the Father, and therefore reigns with Christ on His throne. (For more info on v.28, see supplements.)

Noticeably, after God the Father gives back Christ's Kingdom (v.24) to Christ, Christ can do whatever he wants with it because God the Father is not legally responsible for it (v.27). Therefore, given that it is Christ's creation, Christ can,

> "5 **given it unto whom it seemed meet unto Me [Christ].**" Jeremiah 27:5

And in this case, after Christ receives His Kingdom from God the Father, Christ gives and shares His creation with God the Father and with God the Holy Spirit. And when God the Father joins in to reign (Matthew 6:10) with Christ, Jesus Christ the LORD will be acknowledged first and foremost because all things evolve around Christ the LORD of hosts.

Therefore, as an example, when you and I pray, we pray to God the Father in the name of Jesus Christ

Claiming Sovereignty

the LORD. We do not exclude Jesus Christ the LORD from our prayers; we put Christ first in our prayers. Everything is done in the name of Jesus Christ. And without Jesus Christ nothing can be done. Jesus said, "without Me ye [all of you] can do nothing" (John 15:5).

And to further confirm the fact that Christ the LORD of hosts is the sovereign God of "all things," Jesus said,

> "6 I am the way, the truth, and the life: no man cometh unto the Father, but by Me" (John 14:6).

Did you hear that?

Christ the LORD said, "no man cometh unto the Father, but by Me."

As per the above brief presentation, if you choose to exclude Jesus Christ the LORD of hosts, and go directly to God the Father, or to some other god, your prayer and recognition will not be accepted by God the Father or by God the Holy Spirit. In fact, even Christ the LORD of hosts will also alienate Himself from you, if you willfully bypass Christ and don't want to recognize His absolute Sovereignty.

Although you might chose not to recognize Christ's Sovereignty, the host of heaven recognizes His Sovereignty; and therefore they worship Him.

Nehemiah writes:

> "6 Thou [You] even thou, art LORD alone; thou [You] hast made heaven, the heaven of heavens, with all their host, the earth, and all things that are therein, the seas, and all that is therein, and

Claiming Sovereignty

thou preservest them all; and the host of heaven worshippeth thee [You]." Nehemiah 9:6

These heavenly angels go out of their way to encourage us today to worship Christ the LORD God of Abraham by,

"7 Saying with a loud voice, Fear God, and give glory to Him; for the hour of His judgment is come: and worship Him [Christ] that made heaven, and earth, and the sea, and the fountains of waters." Revelation 14:7

Consequently, you can agree or disagree with the above heavenly host and with the angels who admonish us to worship Christ the LORD of hosts. But, if you disagree, I have to ask, to who in the heavens are you going to compare Christ the LORD of hosts and bypass Him?

The Psalmist asks that very same question,

"6 For who in the heaven can be compared unto the LORD [Christ v.8]? who among the sons of the mighty can be likened unto the LORD?" (Psalms 89:6).

Furthermore, if you cannot find anyone in heaven to compare Jesus Christ the LORD of hosts, where are you going to find a greater God than Christ the LORD of hosts to compare Him to, or to avoid worshipping Him?

The apostle of the LORD writes:

Claiming Sovereignty

> "13 For when God [Christ] made promise to Abraham, because He could swear by no greater, He sware by Himself." Hebrews 6:13

So! Where are you going to find somebody greater that Jesus Christ the LORD of hosts?

If you claim that you can find somebody, in the Bible, greater than Christ the LORD of hosts, please write to me; I would like to know, who is that individual?

Noticeably, I cannot find such an individual in the entire sixty-six book of the Bible!

But, if you are unable to find somebody greater than Christ the LORD of hosts, at the end, as per Scripture, Christ the God of Abraham and of Israel will still uphold and maintain His Sovereign stance by saying to you and to me,

> "5 I am the LORD, and there is none else, there is no God beside Me:" Isaiah 45:5

As a result, the final conclusion is simple; there is no greater God than Jesus Christ the LORD of hosts. There is no other Sovereign God beside Jesus Christ the LORD of hosts who can claim superiority over Christ or over the "all things," which Jesus Christ the LORD has created for Himself and by Himself. Therefore, Christ must be acknowledged that He is the supreme Sovereign God of "all things." And, if you do not want to acknowledge that fact right now, sooner or later you will because Scripture tells us that every knee will bow down before Christ the LORD of hosts, and

Christ's Sovereignty……….. *By: Philip Mitanidis*
Claiming Sovereignty

acknowledge Him as the supreme Sovereign LORD God of "all things," which He has created by Himself and for Himself.

-OOO-

Christ said, "4 command them [the deligates who came to Jerusalem] to say unto their masters, Thus saith the LORD of hosts, the God of Israel; Thus shall ye say unto your masters;

"5 I have made the earth, the man and the beast that are upon the ground, by My great power and by My outstretched arm, and have given it unto whom it seemed meet unto Me." Jeremiah 27:4, 5

SUPPLEMENTS

1 Corinthians 15:28

Contrary to Scripture, the three humongous religious institutions (Muslims, Jews, Christians) believe that all of the Old Testament prophets wrote, in one form or another, about God the Father. Therefore these three religious institutions disagree with Jesus Christ the LORD of hosts when He said to His tempters,

> "45 Do not think that I will accuse you to the Father: there is one that accuseth you, even Moses, in whom ye [all of you] trust.
>
> "46 For had ye [all of you] believed Moses, ye would have believed Me: for
>
> "he wrote of Me.
>
> "47 But if ye believe not his writings, how shall ye believe My words?" John 5:45-47

Furthermore, in reference to the Old Testament, again Jesus Christ the LORD also stated to His tempters that not only Moses wrote about Him but that the rest of the prophets of old wrote about Him. He said to them,

> "39 Search the scriptures; for in them ye [all of you] think ye have eternal life:

and they are they which testify of Me" (John 5:39).

Jesus states clearly in the above verse that the (OT) Scriptures "testify of Me [Him]."

By rejecting Christ's above words that the Old Testament is about Him, these three humongous religious institutions not only disagree with Christ the LORD, as the House of Judah did 2,000 years ago, but they insist that the Old Testament refers to God the Father as the all powerful almighty God, and somehow claim that Christ is subservient to him.

And for that reason they refer to Jesus Christ the LORD of hosts as a prophet, a good man, a philanthropist, a created being, a philosopher, etc., etc. And therefore because of their demeaning misrepresentation of Jesus Christ the LORD, they think that it justifies the changes they have made in various Bible translations. These willful changes to the Bible verses are deliberately made; they are made to reflect their beliefs, which are contrary to the original wording in the Hebrew and in the Greek texts. I make that statement because the translators want these changes to reflect their religious doctrine. And the other reason the translators make willful changes to the Bible verses is due to the fact that they want to publish another newly translated Bible; and when they do, they have to alter minimum of ten percent of the verses of the Bible to read differently from the original verses and from the thousands of mistranslated already published Bibles, in order to avoid copyrights infringements.

Very drastic changes, don't you think?

According to Jesus, changing or deleting one

Christ's Sovereignty.......... By: Philip Mitanidis
1 Corinthians 15:22-28

iota or tittle is bad enough, how much more changing or deleting ten percent of the words of the Bible, every time a new translation is printed, in order to avoid prosecution because of copyrights?

A lot more can be said about the number of altered verses that are made in the various Bibles; and about the willful changes to the Bible verses that are made by the translators of various religious denominations, in order to reflect their religious doctrinal beliefs; but because the task is huge, I will let you do the math as to how many Bible verses have been altered by adding words to the verses or taking words away from the verses. And one of those verses, which they added words and deleted words, is found in 1 Corinthians 15:28.

The verse reads as follows:

> "$_{28}$ And when all things shall be subdued unto Him [Christ], then shall the Son also himself be subject unto him that put all things under Him, that God may be all in all." 1 Corinthians 15:28

Since the three conglomerate religious institutions make God the Father the predominate figure of the Godhead, they use the above mistranslated verse to portray Christ as the Individual who is subjected to God the Father.

But is that what the Greek text says?

Let us look at the references and conceder them in the Greek text.

Apostle Paul writes:

Christ's Sovereignty……….. *By: Philip Mitanidis*
1 Corinthians 15:28

"22 For as in Adam all die, even so in Christ shall all be made alive. 23 But every man in his own order: Christ the firstfruits; afterward they that are Christ's at His coming.

"24 Then cometh the end, when he shall have delivered up the kingdom to God [τω Θεω], even the Father; when he shall have put down all rule and all authority and power.

"25 For he must reign, till he hath put all enemies under His feet.

"26 The last enemy that shall be destroyed is death. 27 For he hath put all things under His feet. But when he saith all things are put under Him, it is manifest that he is excepted, which did put all things under Him.

"28 And when all things shall be subdued unto Him, then shall the Son also himself be subject unto him that put all things under Him, that God may be all in all." 1 Corinthians 15:22-28

In the above verses, Apostle Paul describes the transition that is going to take place in regards to Christ's Kingdom (the "all things") between God the Christ and God the Father.

Apostle Paul begins by saying, in Adam all die, and in Christ they shall be made alive (v.22). And then he says that every one in their order. Christ the first fruit will be resurrected first and then, they at His coming (v.23). But before Christ comes the second time

Christ's Sovereignty.......... *By: Philip Mitanidis* 203
1 Corinthians 15:22-28

to take His penitent people to heaven, God the Father will deliver God's Kingdom (τω Θεω) after he puts "down all rule and all authority and power" (v.24). And when God the Father subdues and puts all of Christ's enemies under Christ's feet (v.25; Psalms 110:1), God the Father will stop reigning and will give all power and authority to Jesus Christ the LORD (v.25). Christ comes to earth with His holy angels to resurrect His saints and takes them with the living saint to heaven. After that, God the Father subjects and gives back Christ's Kingdom to Christ. Inturn, Jesus Christ subjects "28 all things under Him [God the Father], that God may be all in all" (1 Corinthians 15:28).

Therefore, by Christ subjecting His Kingdom (all things) to God the Father, God the Father is not excluded (v.27) from Christ's Kingdom. Instead, he will reign with Christ on His throne (v.28).

Having said that, the three massive religious institutions (Muslims, Jews, and Christians), will argue and state, over and over again that the verse in 1 Corinthians 15:28 states explicitly that after God the Father subjects all things to Christ, then Christ and the "all things" will be subjected to God the Father.

Many in these humongous religious institutions quote their favorite mistranslated Bible verses, and others quote their favorite prophets, in order to support their stand that Christ will subject Himself unto God the Father. And to support their belief, you will find one of those mistranslated verses comes not only from the (OKJV) of the Bible, but from many other mistranslated Bibles that are thriving in the market place. In favor of their argument, this is how the mistranslated verse reads,

Christ's Sovereignty .... *By: Philip Mitanidis*
1 Corinthians 15:28

"28 And when all things shall be subdued unto Him, then shall the Son also himself be subject unto him that put all things under Him, that God may be all in all." 1 Corinthians 15:28

But, to their displeasure, the verse in the Greek text states otherwise. It states that Christ will subject to God the Father that which was subjected to Him by God the Father, mainly the "all things," which Jesus Christ the LORD had already subjected to God the Father before He came in the flesh, on earth, to be crucified on your behalf and mine. In confirmation, here is how the Greek text from a modern translation reads,

"28 Οταν δε υποταχθωσιν εις αυτον τα παντα, τοτε και αυτος ο Υιος θελει υποταχθη εις τον υποταξαντα εις αυτον τα παντα, δια να ηναι ο Θεος τα παντα εν πασι." ΠΡΟΣ ΚΟΡΙΝΘΙΟΥΣ Α' ΚΕΘ. ιε 28. Η Αγια Γραφη, Βιβλικη Εταιρεια, Αθηναι, 1961. 1 Corinthians 15:28

And when we strip some of the added words from the above modern translation, we can see that it is compatible with another version, which reads as follows,

"28 οταν δε υποταγη αυτω τα παντα τοτε και αυτος ο υιος υποταγησεται τω υποταξαντι αυτω τα παντα ινα η ο Θεος παντα εν πασιν" (1 Corinthians 15:28). Diaglott

Christ's Sovereignty.......... *By: Philip Mitanidis*
1 Corinthians 15:22-28

    To translate the above verse into English, the second, fifth, eighth, and eleventh line will read word for word, as close as possible, as follows,

1. line "28 οταν δε υποταγη αυτω τα παντα,
2. line   when   subjects to Him the   all things,
3. OKJV "28 And when all things shall be subdued unto Him [Christ],"

4.   τοτε και αυτος ο   υιος υποταγησεται
5.   then and He   the   Son subjects
6. OKJV then shall the Son also himself be subject

7.   τω υποταξαντι   αυτω τα παντα,
8.   to   the subjector, to Him the   all things
9. OKJV unto him that put all things under Him,

10.   ινα   η   ο Θεος   παντα   εν πασιν."
11.   maybe   the God   all things in all.
12. OKJV that   God may be all   in all."
1 Corinthians 15:28

    As a result, if you look at the first line of the old Greek text and compare it with the 3rd line, it has been translated in an unorthodox manner, into English, by the (OKJV) correctly, right up until the word "Him" (αυτω).

    "28 And when all things shall be subdued unto Him,"

    The reason I have stated line three is translated into English in an unorthodox manner is due to the fact

Christ's Sovereignty .... *By: Philip Mitanidis*
1 Corinthians 15:28

when you look at the words in line two they do not make sense grammatically. Therefore to have a rational constructive sentence in English, which makes sense, a person has to juggle the English words a bit or a lot in some cases. And this verse is one of those cases.

Therefore, when you consider the Greek text (1st line) with the English text (3rd line), you will notice, the English text (OKJV) has added and rearranged a number of words in the verse. It reads,

1. line "28 οταν δε υποταγη αυτω τα παντα,
2. line   when   subjects   to Him   the   all things,
3. OKJV "28 And when all things shall be subdued unto Him [Christ],"

But, line three should read more precisely, "When subdued to Him [Christ] the all things,"

When you compare line three with line two, you can plainly see that the word "And" in the beginning of the sentence has been added by the (OKJV). Like-wise, the words from line three ("when all things shall be") are also added in between the words "when" and "subjects" or subdued if you like? And the words "unto Him" are placed on the end of the sentence; whereby, in the Greek sentence, "the all things" are placed at the end of the sentence.

Although the words have been rearranged in the English translation, by the (OKJV), the sentence manages to read comparatively correct. It reads,

3. OKJV "28 And when all things shall be subdued unto Him [Christ],"

Christ's Sovereignty......... *By: Philip Mitanidis*
1 Corinthians 15:22-28

But, as I stated before, line three should read more precisely, "When subdued to Him [Christ] the all things."

So, what happens "28 when all things shall be subdued unto Him [Christ]"?

To get an answer, you will find when you consider the 6th line of the (OKJV), and compare it to the Greek text (4th line), it becomes very messy. You can readily notice the added and deleted and rearranged words in the (OKJV). Therefore, in line six, I have turned the uninspired added words into italics for your convenience.

4. τοτε και αυτος ο υιος υποταγησεται
5. then and He the Son subjects
6. OKJV then *shall* the Son *also himself be* subject

7. τω υποταξαντι αυτω τα παντα,
8. to the subjector to Him the all things
9. OKJV unto him that put all things under Him."

As you can readily see, the words from line four and five do not correspond with the uninspired added words *"shall"* and *"also himself,"* in line six. Likewise lines seven and eight do not correspond to line nine. Line six and line nine should read,

"then and He the Son subjects
to the subjector to Him the all things."

And why does Jesus Christ subject "all things," which He had created back to God the Father, after God the Father subjects "all things" to Christ?

Christ's Sovereignty.......... *By: Philip Mitanidis*
1 Corinthians 15:28

The answer is given because Christ wants to ("θελει." Βιβλικη Εταιρεια); and as per line 12, so "that God may be all in all."

10.	ινα	η	ο Θεος	παντα	εν	πασιν."
11.	maybe		the God	all things	in	all.
12. OKJV	that		God may be all		in	all."

1 Corinthians 15:28

Therefore because Christ the LORD subjects "all things" back to God the Father, God the Father is not excluded from reigning with Christ the LORD of hosts over Christ's Kingdom.

As per the above presentation, God the Father is going to return (subject) "all things" unto Jesus Christ the LORD (v.28), after he subdues Christ's enemies and puts them under Christ's feet (Psalms 110:1). And when he puts Christ's enemies under Christ's feet, God the Father stops reigning and Christ begins to reign. And while Christ's enemies are under His feet, Christ comes to planet earth with His angels to resurrect His dead saints and take them with the living saints to heaven. And while they are all in heaven, the transition of Christ's Kingdom takes place. God the Father returns "all things" to Christ, And during His reign, Christ subjects "all things," which God the Father subjected to Christ back to God the Father (v.28) so that God the Father is not excluded (v.27) from "all things," which Jesus Christ the LORD of hosts created "by Himself" and "for Himself."

Please note, as per the Greek text, what is subjected between God the Father and Jesus Christ the LORD is "all things," which Christ created.

Christ's Sovereignty.......... *By: Philip Mitanidis*
1 Corinthians 15:22-28

Therefore, we can conclude that God the Father is not part of the "all things" subjected to Jesus Christ; and neither is Jesus Christ the LORD of hosts part of the "all things" that are subjected to God the Father.

Take a good look at verse twenty-eight again.

As you can see, the verse does not state in the Greek text that Christ Himself is going to be subjected to God the Father. The words "Himself," and "also," as you can readily see, in the Greek text, do not exist in verse twenty-eight.

Therefore we have to conclude, since the translators of the (OKJV) have added, deleted, and rearranged words in v.28, we can safely say that the verse in 1 Corinthians 15:28 is mistranslated in the (OKJV) of the Bible.

Consequently the verse, as per lines 2, 5, 8, and 11 should read close to the following,

"28 And when all things shall be subdued unto Him [Christ], then, and He the Son subjects unto the subjector to Him the all things that God maybe all in all." Corinthians 15:28

QUESTIONS

1). How many Gods are mentioned in the Trinitarian doctrine?
2). a) Name the three Trinitarian Gods by their character names. b) What are their surnames?
3). Who created "all things"?
4). Was there more than one Creator involved in the creation of "all things"?
5). What are the "all things" that were created.
6). How long did it take to create the ecosystem of the earth, man, animals, birds, etc., etc.
7). For whom were the "all things" created?
8). Who is the owner of the "all things" that were created?
9). Who is the Sovereign God of "all things" that were created?
10). When the prophets of old refer to "the Kingdom of God," to what Kingdom and God are they referring to?
11). Whose administration is implemented in the Kingdom of God?
12). Who says, "there is not god beside Me"?
13). Why does He say, "there is no God beside Me"?
14). Which one of the three Gods of the Bible is the God of Abraham and of Israel?
15). Who took the children of Israel out of Egypt, and led them into the Promised Land?
16). a) Who came from heaven to die on Calvary's cross? b) Why did He do that?

Christ's Sovereignty.......... *By: Philip Mitanidis* 211
Questions

17). Before He came to planet earth to die on Calvary's cross, what did He do with His Kingdom (the "all things," which He created)?
18). Today, who has custody over His Kingdom?
19). a) Is His Kingdom going to be given back to Him? b) When?
20). After He receives His kingdom, what is He going to do with it?
21). Why is He going to share His Kingdom with the other two Associates (Gods)?

www.ingramcontent.com/pod-product-compliance
Lightning Source LLC
Chambersburg PA
CBHW061641040426
42446CB00010B/1524